LORD, I'M YOURS

LORD, I'M YOURS

Devotions for College Students

Gary P. Baumler

NORTHWESTERN PUBLISHING HOUSE
Milwaukee, Wisconsin

Library of Congress Card 86-62761
Northwestern Publishing House
1250 N. 113th St., P.O. Box 26975, Milwaukee, WI 53226-0975
© 1987 by Northwestern Publishing House.
Published 1987
Printed in the United States of America
ISBN 0-8100-0256-6

TO MY SONS DAN AND BRENT

May they, like Job,
continue constant in prayer and
live for the life to come.

The Teacher of Ecclesiastes gave the impetus for a book like this when he advised, "Remember your Creator in the days of your youth, before the days of trouble come and the years approach when you will say, 'I find no pleasure in them.' "

Some wit in more recent years, catching a bit of the Teacher's meaning, put it this way: "We get too soon old and too late smart." And virtually all of us over thirty, or forty, as the case may be, look back upon our youth knowing exactly what the two messages mean.

Youth is an island someplace between puberty and parity where a person goes to enjoy life while looking for the most promising bridge to a still better life — for everyone must, sooner or later, leave the island. While on the island, the young grow restless — sometimes for a return to the more protected days of childhood, sometimes for the world that waits in the obscure future, sometimes for the elusive realities of youth itself.

Those who know say, "Don't waste your youth," or "Don't rush to leave it behind." Many offer advice, good and bad, about making the most of one's youth.

We agree with the words of caution: "Don't waste . . . ." "Don't rush . . . ." We repeat the advice of the Teacher: "Remember your Creator in the days of your youth . . . ." May God be with you and bless you, not only in the days of your youth, but all your days.

CONTENTS

x

CONTENTS (contd.)

SERIES THREE: LORD, I'M ON THE WAY

Series One
Lord, I'm Suffering

1. HELP ME BE LIKE JOB

In the land of Uz there lived a man whose name was Job. This man was blameless and upright; he feared God and shunned evil. He had seven sons and three daughters, and he owned seven thousand sheep, three thousand camels, five hundred yoke of oxen and five hundred donkeys, and had a large number of servants. He was the greatest man among all the people of the East.

His sons used to take turns holding feasts in their homes, and they would invite their three sisters to eat and drink with them. When a period of feasting had run its course, Job would send and have them purified. Early in the morning he would sacrifice a burnt offering for each of them, thinking, "Perhaps my children have sinned and cursed God in their hearts." This was Job's regular custom. (Job 1:1-5)

Let me introduce you to a man who can teach you a lot about belonging to God and living for God, no matter what happens in your life. Come and see a man whose life can give meaning to your life as you begin to identify with him. Our text has introduced him simply as "a man whose name was Job."

We shall learn to know Job as a man unique among men, the kind of person you and I wish we could be. Paradoxically, we shall see him also as a kind of "everyman" — someone with whom each of us can and will identify, the kind of person you and I may pity, if we do not scorn.

To begin to get a picture of Job, just envision the kind of person you think would fit your ideal of an outstanding member for your church, maybe even an outstanding pastor. No, Job wasn't a pastor, but he had the qualities we might like to see in one. He was a leader among men, and

3

to describe Job's character is to describe what great men of the church are made of.

Job was pious without being a pietist, religious without being a legalist. He avoided evil without spoiling fun. As a father, he involved his children in the true worship of the Lord. At the same time he encouraged them to enjoy life. We read, "This man was blameless and upright; he feared God and shunned evil. . . . He was the greatest man among all the people of the East."

The Job we meet here is almost too good to be true. He is the kind of person that you and I should try to emulate, for he has the qualities we expect to find in great men of faith.

But who can do it? Who can live up to these standards?

The Bible calls Job "blameless and upright." Even if "blameless" does not mean the same thing as sinless, can any one of us qualify? The word "blameless" has to do with maturity and completeness. Today we might call Job a complete Christian, someone mature in the faith, whose whole heart belongs to God. Maybe it doesn't mean sinless, but doesn't "blameless and upright" still seem out of our reach?

Do you *fear God and shun evil* as Job did? This doesn't mean most of the time, but all of the time. This means, for example, that you turn off all TV programs that promote immorality and trash and stay away from movies that do the same. Do you? Job would have.

Is Job, then, too much the ideal man for you to identify with him? Although sometimes it may seem that your parents and professors expect you to be like Job, that's just not realistic.

Maybe so.

Nevertheless, we believe and hope you will strive to be like Job. We reason so because Someone who was blameless in the full sense of being sinless has already walked the road for you; because that One, your Savior Jesus, knew you must fail whenever the ideal is held before you and, therefore, suffered and died for your failures; because that same Jesus has promised you his Spirit and asked that you live by his Spirit. In the Spirit of Jesus, Job's ideal will have meaning for you.

5

Today we have only briefly met him. In succeeding devotions we hope you will learn some good things from him and that you will grow in the desire to be ever more like the "man whose name was Job."

Dear God, our Lord and Savior, we all know that we ought to live according to the ideal pattern we learn from Job. But, knowing our own weaknesses, we call upon you by the Spirit of your Son to give us the strength and purpose we need to persevere, and, for the sake of your Son, we ask you to forgive us when we fall short. We pray in Jesus' name. Amen.

2. HELP ME RESIST SATAN

One day the angels came to present themselves before the LORD, and Satan also came with them. The LORD said to Satan, "Where have you come from?"

Satan answered the LORD, "From roaming through the earth and going back and forth in it."

Then the LORD said to Satan, "Have you considered my servant Job? There is no one on earth like him; he is blameless and upright, a man who fears God and shuns evil."

"Does Job fear God for nothing?" Satan replied. "Have you not put a hedge around him and his household and everything he has? You have blessed the

work of his hands, so that his flocks and herds are spread throughout the land. But stretch out your hand and strike everything he has, and he will surely curse you to your face."

6

The LORD said to Satan, "Very well, then, everything he has is in your hands, but on the man himself do not lay a finger."

Then Satan went out from the presence of the LORD. (Job 1:6-12)

This is a multiple choice test. Pick the best answer:

1. a) There is no sin in our church.
   b) There should be no sin in our church.
   c) We don't have to worry about sin in our church.
2. a) Temptations abound in our church.
   b) There are few temptations in our church.
   c) It is easy to avoid temptations in our church.

If, like me, you don't particularly like any of the choices, then try to imagine the following scene taking place sometime in the history of our church:

Satan, fresh from spreading his evil ways over the earth, appears in the presence of the Lord. The Lord speaks to Satan: "Have you considered my servants in that small conservative Lutheran church? In all the earth there are none more upright, dedicated to do the work of God, versed in and living by the word of God."

"Ha!" Satan replies. "What does that mean? Have you fenced them in with a comfortable ring of orthodoxy, made them happy with their strong synodical ties and content in their potluck dinners? Stretch out your hand to test them, expose them to the world, disturb them at their tasks, and they will surely scoff at your ways and ignore your word."

The Lord says to Satan, "Very well then, have your way and put them to the test."

The scene we just imagined parallels closely the scene in our text which actually took place long ago in connection with the "man whose name was Job." And we should be sure to observe certain similarities to our situation:

To begin with, God identified Job as his servant. In our church we firmly believe that we are all servants of God and we look for ways to serve him.

Furthermore, Job appeared to be protected by God and made to prosper so that it was quite easy for him to serve God. Our church with its Bible-centered theology and careful attention to scriptural detail appears to be protected and successful so that we may find it quite easy to serve God in the church.

Finally, the devil wanted to turn Job away from God and was allowed to do his worst to make Job curse God. Likewise, the devil wants to turn us away from God and will do his worst to make us scoff at the Lord.

Make no mistake, Satan is active among us and the people of our church. If you attend church to escape his evil ways, you had better know he won't let you off that easily. If you join a congregation expecting not to see any of the results of his work, prepare yourself for some shocks and some trials, and pray that God will give you some of the strengths of a Job.

Satan means "adversary" and he is that to us. He is not the Satan whom *Newsweek* magazine once offered to give us "a new look at" and identified as just another mythical figure, a "Symbol of evil" (an inadequate one at that), and a "trivial personification."

That "trivial personification" in the form of a serpent brought the taste of hell to paradise and plunged all human-kind under the curse of sin. That "trivial personification" has destroyed countless souls by his wiles and even tested the Lord Jesus himself. Do you think Job's friends would have helped him in his trials more if only they had convinced him that Satan was just a "trivial personification"?

No, Satan is an evil spirit who wanders over this earth "like a roaring lion looking for someone to devour" (1 Peter 5:8).

So, how can we escape? How can we continue to be faithful servants of God if Satan is so active against us? Answer: the same way Job would have to do it when the devil turned on him. Job's faith would have to withstand the test. Peter wrote, "Resist him [Satan], standing firm in the faith" (1 Peter 5:9). Luther said, "One little word can fell him."

Like Job, we can make it by the faith worked in us by God's Word. The Word points us to Jesus, who rejected all of Satan's temptations leveled at him, who endured the very pangs of Satan's hell and then rose victorious from the dead, with whom we are safe no matter what the devil can do, and from whom we get the power to withstand.

Now then, in your daily life, even in your church life, don't be shocked when you encounter the workings of Satan, but rather be ready to "resist him, standing firm in the faith."

O God of power and might, protect and keep me on my way so that Satan may not have his way with me, for Jesus' sake. Amen.

3. HELP ME COPE WITH TRAGEDY

(Three messengers have just reported tragedies which wiped out Job's wealth.) **While he was still speaking, yet another messenger came and said, "Your sons and daughters were feasting and drinking wine at the oldest brother's house, when suddenly a mighty wind swept in from the desert and struck the**

four corners of the house. It collapsed on them and they are dead, and I am the only one who has escaped to tell you!"

At this, Job got up and tore his robe and shaved his head. Then he fell to the ground in worship and said: "Naked I came from my mother's womb, and naked I will depart. The LORD gave and the LORD has taken away; may the name of the LORD be praised."

9

In all this, Job did not sin by charging God with wrongdoing. (Job 1:18-22)

Something frightening has been happening in our country in recent years, something hard to deal with. Without much warning companies that were large and prosperous have laid off large numbers of workers for an indefinite period. In some cases they have shut down altogether, for good.

Have you ever stopped to consider what happens to the families involved? We see people out of work, out of money and out of hope, people plunging from prosperity to poverty almost overnight. And, speaking of plunging, remember how some who lost their jobs and their fortunes in the Great Depression committed suicide by jumping from tall buildings.

How do you cope when your world seems to be collapsing around you?

How does one cope in the face of tragedy?

During a visit at one of our Lutheran high schools I was talking with a secretary of the school. "One day," she said, after I had referred to a tragedy in the life of a mutual friend, "my husband backed the car out of our garage not knowing that our 1½ year-old son had crawled under the car."

I still recall vividly the night only a short time later, when my mother called to tell me that a woman with whom I was confirmed in more carefree days had lost her only daughter — a teenager — in a freak auto accident. Only two years earlier she had lost her only son — a teenager — in a freak accident.

How do such people cope?

When we think of the difficulty we sometimes have just coping with life in general — with our studies, with our social lives, with our teachers, with our emotions — that's an important question. I know how horror-struck I felt when I heard about the infant crushed under the car driven by his own father. How do you suppose the father and mother felt?

Of course, these are not new problems. In this life people often have to cope with suffering and sorrow. It happened to the man named Job, whom we are beginning to get to know. He lived so long ago that we may feel far removed from his tragedy. We may not be moved when we hear how Job, who had so much, lost everything he possessed. He lost a fortune to bandits and to natural disaster. He lost all ten of his children in a devastating tornado. The man whom Satan accused God of protecting on all sides suddenly felt the crushing blows of destruction on all sides. Someone who has just lost his job even as he is mourning a death may begin to understand how Job felt.

How did Job cope?

He did not commit suicide. He did not turn suddenly bitter and curse God as Satan had predicted he would. He responded in faith. Oh, he demonstrated a deep sense of anguish, sorrow and humility, as in typical eastern fashion he "tore his robe and shaved his head," but then "he fell to the ground in worship."

Instead of curses, his mouth uttered praises. God had given him his riches. God had given him his children. Now God had let him lose both. All earthly treasures come and go, but only God endures forever. We bring nothing into the world, we shall take nothing out. But God will provide while we are here. Praise be to God! "May the name of the LORD be praised."

10

Job coped because Job trusted God. That's also how Christians to this day are coping, including the women we have mentioned who lost their children. That's how we can cope in the face of all difficulties.

We have a God who gave up the riches of heaven so that we might receive those riches. Trust in him when the riches of this life are taken away. We have a Friend and Brother who, though he died, lives to welcome us into the family in heaven. Trust in him even if you lose your earthly family now. We have a Savior who experienced hell to save the world. Trust in him when this world seems like hell.

"May the name of the LORD be praised."

O God, we trust your name; we praise your name. Be with us, O Lord, for your name's sake. Amen.

4. HELP ME UNDERSTAND THE HUMAN CONDITION

After this, Job opened his mouth and cursed the day of his birth.

"Why did I not perish at birth, and die as I came from the womb?"

"Or why was I not hidden in the ground like a stillborn child, like an infant who never saw the light of day?"

"Why is light given to those in misery, and life to the bitter of soul . . .?"

"Why is life given to a man whose way is hidden, whom God has hedged in?"

"I have no peace, no quietness; I have no rest, but only turmoil." (Job 3:1, 11, 16, 20, 23, 26)

Satan was not yet finished with the man whose name was Job. He had already worked destruction against Job on all sides. Job had lost all his possessions. He had endured the death of his ten children in one tragic calamity. But still he had praised the name of the Lord.

Now Satan afflicted Job in his own body, reasoning that if God let Job suffer in his own flesh and bones, Job would then surely curse God. So Satan "afflicted Job with painful sores from the soles of his feet to the top of his head" (2:7). Some have conjectured that this was the very worst kind of leprosy. It got so bad that Job's wife, playing into the devil's hands, finally scolded Job, "Are you still holding on to your integrity? Curse God and die!" (2:9).

Neverthless Job remained constant, saying, "You are talking like a foolish woman. Shall we accept good from God, and not trouble?" (2:10).

When three close friends of Job heard about his troubles, they came to visit him. They could hardly recognize him at first because the sores had so badly disfigured him. They wept aloud at the sight, tore their robes and sprinkled dust on their heads.

Seven days later Job broke a protracted silence and actually complained about his lot. Yes, and he did more. He cursed the day he was born. "He said: 'May the day of my birth perish, and the night it was said, "A boy is born!" ' " (3:3). The blameless and upright Job had begun to bend under the burden. This model of patient endurance was showing human weakness.

In some ways it's almost a relief to hear him. He is human after all. If you wanted to be like him, he was almost too good to be true — too much unlike us for us even to try to be like him. But now he comes down to earth. He asks with the rest of us the unanswerable question: "Why? If life is the pits, why do we have to live? Why?" He lays bare his soul and reveals the kind of struggle that goes on inside many a sufferer.

Job has asked the question, and for the moment we hear no answer but the haunting echo of his cry in our own subconscious. He has touched on the mystery of our being, and he leaves us fearing there is no more to say. We have witnessed a low point and heard a man experiencing extreme despair. As if in an O'Neill play, Job seems to be taking "a long day's journey into night."

We need to search further to find some light to shed on this dark scene, and we shall. But for now, let's take the moment to see what we have found here in the darkness. Job has given us a firsthand look at the human condition in this world corrupted by sin. It's not a pretty sight — emptiness, weariness, helplessness, the very bottom of the pit. Even the best — and in human terms Job is the best — are caught up in this condition and must pay the price for just being born.

But instead of turning our heads away in revulsion and driving from our minds the inevitability of it all, let us rather face what we see and grow in understanding of what else we know. From the perspective of Job's despair we may learn to appreciate the more what our Savior had to endure when he took our place in suffering.

Remember Job and understand why one greater than Job would so fervently pray in the Garden of Gethsemane that the Father might let the cup of suffering pass from him. Jesus was not merely apprehensive of being beaten and crucified. He was preparing himself to experience the worst of what I have called "the human condition," "the bottom of the pit." Remember Job and realize how inevitable it was that Jesus, as Job's and our Substitute, must at last cry from the cross, "My God, my God, *why* have you forsaken me?" (Matthew 27:46).

And, even as we are looking past Job to Jesus, remember that "Jesus" is the answer to Job's question. "Jesus, Jesus, only Jesus!"

14

> Jesus, Jesus, only Jesus,
> > Can my heartfelt longing still.
> Lo, I pledge myself to Jesus
> > What he wills alone to will.
> For my heart which he hath filled,
> > Ever cries, Lord, as thou wilt. Amen.

5. HELP ME FIND A TRUE FRIEND

(Job's friend Eliphaz is advising Job.)

"Your words have supported those who stumbled; you have strengthened faltering knees. But now trouble comes to you, and you are discouraged; it strikes you, and you are dismayed."

"Consider now: Who, being innocent, has ever perished? Where were the upright ever destroyed? As I have observed, . . . those who sow trouble reap it."

"Resentment kills a fool, and envy slays the simple."

"Yet man is born to trouble as surely as sparks fly upward. But if it were I, I would appeal to God; I would lay my cause before him."

"Blessed is the man whom God corrects; so do not despise the discipline of the Almighty." (Job 4:4, 5, 7, 8; 5:2, 7, 8, 17)

What do you say to someone who is suffering?

Your friend has just been dropped by his girlfriend. Do you say, "Don't worry you'll get over it in time"? or, "If you would just get your act together, this wouldn't have happened"?

Your friend has been crippled for life in a freak accident. Do you say, "At least you're still alive"? or, "I know exactly how you feel"? or, "You could have avoided the accident if you had only taken a simple safety precaution"?

Your friend has lost a loved one in death. Do you say, "I don't know why he had to go that way"? or, "Isn't it wonderful she lived for 80 years"? or, "At least he went fast"? Or what?

I think we have all been there, If not, we will be sooner or later — either looking for the right words to comfort a friend who is troubled, or feeling troubled and listening to a friend trying to find the right words to say to us. Often, no matter what we say or hear, it seems wrong. We may speak true words, even wise words, meant-to-be-sympathetic words, but they don't seem to help when spoken. They lack real comfort.

The man whose name was Job experienced this very problem. He had troubles. Oh, did he have troubles! And he had friends. They came to him when they heard. They stayed with him and grieved for him. But they didn't really know what to say.

Today we have heard from the first of Job's friends, Eliphaz. We've heard a curious mixture of wisdom and thoughtlessness — sympathy and heartlessness — advice and impertinence.

"You have helped others," he told Job. "Why can't you help yourself?" "Follow your own advice. Practice what you preach." Good advice to this day for anyone who promotes Christian living. If you encourage people to exercise their faith in the face of troubles, learn yourself to exercise your faith in the face of troubles. Good advice, I say, but small comfort when the troubles seem to have taken over your life.

"You reap what you sow," Eliphaz added, implying that Job must have sown the whirlwind. Job must be guilty of some terrible secret sin; otherwise God would not have let him be so sorely afflicted. If he wanted relief, he would have to change his ways. He would have to do something to regain God's favor.

16   Job's friend continued with intended kindness and insensitive inuendo to suggest that Job was a fool, that he had failed to appeal to God as he should, and that he didn't understand what it meant to accept the discipline of the Almighty.

So much for friends and for words of comfort. Eliphaz was an old and wise man. He meant well. But, as so often happens with friends, he didn't really help. Job didn't like what he heard.

What's the point then? What do you say to someone who is suffering?

Why don't you simply say, "You have a Friend. You have a Friend who cares"? But then make sure he or she knows that, although you, too, would like to be such a friend, you mean Friend with a capital *F*. This Friend has walked the path of suffering before you. This Friend stays by your side in the worst going and holds your heart together when otherwise it must break. This Friend asks only that you trust in him as your Friend and Savior, and he will lead you through the very valley of the shadow of death to a joyous feast in glory. This Friend is Jesus. He wants to be your best Friend now and in all eternity.

Oh, Jesus, Friend of sinners and Comforter of sufferers, draw near us in your love. Give rest to us when we feel weary. Calm our hearts when they are troubled. Lead us in the paths of righteousness. Bring us safely through the valleys of sin, tears and death to the heavenly feast at your side in eternity, for your name's sake. Amen.

6. HELP ME STOP COMPLAINING

(Job is speaking.) "The arrows of the Almighty are in me, my spirit drinks in their poison; God's terrors are marshaled against me.

"What is man that you make so much of him, that you give him so much attention, that you examine him every morning and test him every moment? Will you never look away from me, or let me alone even for an instant? If I have sinned, what have I done to you, O watcher of men?" (Job 6:4; 7:17-20)

17

"You're a bully, God." "God, stop picking on me."

Would you ever talk to God that way? I hope not, but I'm not so sure. Oh, of course, you would not likely use words like that, so brasen and crude. You might as well invite God to strike you with lightning. How blasphemous can you get? Imagine — calling God a bully.

But now that brings us back to the man whose name was Job. Do you remember how, when we first met him, we held him up as a model of virtue? "Follow his example," we exhorted, and wondered directly whether any of us could ever really live up to the standards he was setting. Now we see a Job who is altogether too much like us or, at least, a Job whom we may not wish to emulate.

Job comes dangerously close here to calling God a bully. The essence of what he says goes something like this: "Why don't you leave me alone, Lord? Why do you fill me with the arrows of your anger? What could I, a mere man, ever do that could hurt you? Still you watch me constantly and test me. You don't leave me alone long enough to swallow. Sometimes I get the impression that you've set me up like a tin can on a fence and are using me for target practice. Why don't you pick on someone your own size?"

From a tower of strength in the face of adversity, to a man

bent by despair to wish for death, to a complainer who suggests that God can be cruel and mean — Job has appeared to weaken and to begin to self-destruct under Satan's temptations. We, in turn, have applauded Job's strength and identified with his despair. But what now? Do we follow him also in this most recent frame of mind? Do we, like him, ever imply that God is mean or unfair?

What do you think? Look at our record. We often in worship praise God as our "Life," our "Light," and our "Joy"; as our "Shield" and great "Reward"; as the unfailing object of our trust. Each of us holds dearly to the sentiments of David's Good Shepherd Psalm (23). We confess with David, "The Lord leads me. He is at my side. He walks with me, even through the valley of the shadow of death. He serves me in the very presence of my enemies." We have all heard the Great Commission of Jesus and take certain comfort in knowing that he is with us always.

With that kind of company, you would think that we would never have a complaint, wouldn't you? With God leading you by the hand, surely you walk always contented and consoled, don't you? Ideally, yes; but in reality, we sometimes act quite differently.

We become like Job, though we don't suffer nearly as much, and we complain about where God has led us, complain as if he were harassing us instead of helping us, complain as if he were treating us more like an enemy than like a friend. One person complains, "I have to work too hard." Another echoes, "I have to do without so many things." Yet another, "Why can't I be physically stronger? It's not fair." "Why can't the weather be the way I want it?" "I shouldn't have to suffer as I do."

Stop! Don't you see? If you truly believe that God has complete control in your life, then you complain against him when you complain about what he has allowed to happen in your life. You imply that he is mean and unfair.

The next time you feel like complaining, then, bring yourself up short and rather say, "Thank you, God, for staying with me especially when the way is hard. Thank you, God, for assuring me through Jesus that the devil cannot have his way in my life, though he tempts me sorely. Thank you, God, for standing by me even though I sometimes complain. Thank you, God, for the salvation I enjoy through your Son, Jesus Christ."

> O God of grace, each day things happen that make me want to complain, and I often do. Forgive me for such weakness and for what I suggest concerning you by my complaining. Help me rather to remain content wherever you may lead me. Help me to see troubles for what they really are, temptations of Satan and tests of my faith, and to see you for what you are, my help and comfort through troubles and my Savior for an eternity free of troubles. In Jesus' name. Amen.

7. HELP ME ACCEPT YOUR FORGIVENESS

(Job is speaking to God.) "Why do you not pardon my offenses and forgive my sins? For I will soon lie down in the dust; you will search for me, but I will be no more." (Job 7:21)

Once the man named Job has made his impression on our consciousness, we can never forget him. He shows us so much about ourselves. At his best, he shows us what we, too, can become in Christ. At his worst, he gives us a mirror image of our own failings. And we join with him in the struggle that pits our old sinful selves against the man of faith in us.

Today Job appears to ask God for the forgiveness of sins. Well, actually, if you read carefully, you heard him ask God why God did not forgive his sins. Speaking to God he says, "Why do you not forgive my sins, Lord? I'm going to die soon. Then you will seek me to forgive me, but will not find me."

Poor Job! We can hardly imagine how much he suffered, although we know it was enough to make him wish he could die. Then, when he looked for sympathy from his friends, he didn't find any — which was just about the last straw. So now, ironically, he began to share the faulty thinking of his friends.

Job wants forgiveness, if indeed he needs it, although he feels he hasn't really sinned. More to the point, he feels his sufferings prove that God has not forgiven him. Rather, God is displeased with him and therefore is punishing him. He can't understand why God would fail to pardon him. He assumes that forgiveness ought to be unlimited and immediate from God.

Job fell into a trap and we need to take care not to fall in with him. Satan has many tricks to deceive us. The first is just an old song played on a new fiddle. It goes like this: "When you suffer, it means God is punishing you. Only when he is no longer displeased with you will he stop." In other words, you have to earn your forgiveness.

Sufferers beware! You'll find no comfort in this teaching. If you're not suffering at the moment, beware! If you believe Satan's deception, you may lose all comfort the next time you stub your toe.

No matter how you change the tune to suit your own tastes, the result comes out about the same unless you are in tune with God. Job didn't know what to think. On the one hand, he expected God to forgive simply because a human being was not worth condemning. On the other hand, God should forgive because this human being was too worthy to condemn. Finally, and many people today want you to believe this, Job apparently toyed with the idea that God could never bring himself to condemn a helpless human and would err to overlook a good man like Job.

Now, before you pass all this off as the faulty thinking of others, let's remember we all tend to think that way. Someone else falls on bad times, and he or she probably deserved it, was probably out of favor with God. We have troubles, and we don't really deserve them. We feel things must get better because we are who we are. Or when we think of forgiveness, we imagine, "God sees how I've been keeping my nose clean. He'll forgive my faults."

Be careful!

Let's look to God for *his* forgiveness and let nothing obscure his truth. Job came close. He suggested that forgiveness ought to be unlimited and immediate with God. It is — because of God's love, not because of us sinners. Rejoice that we have the New Testament perspective to help us understand that. We don't suffer as a punishment for our sins, because Jesus already suffered our punishment for us. Sure we can still suffer consequences from sinning, just as you can get a stomach ache from eating too much, but we have forgiveness as long as we trust in Jesus. And forgiveness gives comfort that lasts forever, comfort that Job too would discover again before too long. Praise God for forgiveness.

Forgive us, Lord, our sins today and all the days we live. Give us not what we should get, but what you have to give. Give what Jesus earned and promised to us all; give freedom from the curse of sin and save us from the Fall. Amen.

8. HELP ME RISE FROM THE ASHES

(Job is speaking about God.) **"He is not a man like me that I might answer him, that we might confront each other in court. If only there were someone to arbitrate between us, to lay his hand upon us both, someone to remove God's rod from me, so that his terror would frighten me no more. Then I would speak up without fear of him, but as it now stands with me, I cannot." (Job 9:32-35)**

I don't recall that I have ever seen a picture drawn to portray "the man whose name was Job." If ever I do, I expect to see him seated in a pile of ashes. For when he hit bottom in his misery, we are told, ". . . he sat among the ashes." In all the conversation between him and his friends which fills most of the Book of Job, he probably continued to sit there. Furthermore, near the close of the book, after he had resolved his doubts, he said to the Lord, "I repent in dust and ashes."

Job may be the earliest person we know of who used ashes as a sign of sorrow and of repentance, but ashes and Job's reasons for sitting in them are of only secondary importance for the moment. Far more important, Job in his reflections while in the ashes shows us why the passion of the Messiah had to happen.

Still crushed and confused, searching for justice, crying for help, Job outlined what had to happen for a human being to gain a favorable audience with God. Job probably did not foresee the Savior when he spoke at this time, but he saw what a savior would have to accomplish.

Job, you see, knew that he, a mere man, could hardly stand up before God if court were held. "I know," he admitted to God, "you will not hold me innocent." Man can answer to man, Job reasoned, but we need an arbitrator, a public defender, a mediator if we must take the stand before God. We need someone who can identify with and influence both God and man and someone who will "remove God's rod" from us.

Does that sound wonderfully like Someone you and I know? Let the world scoff at the gospel. When a man is down and dying, he cries for what the gospel gives. "Give us relief. Give us a helper, someone to plead our case before God. Give us someone who can lift the heavy hand of God from us, can remove the rod of his punishment."

Have you ever felt that way? I have. Every time God's command says, "Do," but I don't, or says, "Don't," but I do — every time the ravages of this sin-affected age upset my life — every time I'm sick, alone, afraid, helpless, I have wanted to protest to God. I have wanted a savior, an arbitrator, a mediator.

That's what the suffering of Jesus Christ has given us. Jesus, the God-man "identifies with and influences both God and man." He followed the path of our sorrows. He bared his back to the full scourging of God's anger against our sin. He gave his holy life in bloody death to satisfy the penalty God had decreed against us. Because of Jesus' passion, we have "one who speaks to the Father in our defense," a public defender, "Jesus Christ, the Righteous One." (1 John 2:1) Just as there is but one, unapproachable God; so too there is "one mediator between God and men, the man Christ Jesus, who gave himself as a ransom for all men." (1 Timothy 2:5, 6)

Because of Jesus' suffering, we can fear God without being afraid of him. We can find comfort in our troubles. We can rise again from the ashes.

Dear God of mercy, just as the man Job once sat in real ashes, so often we sit figuratively in the ashes of sorrow and repentance as we ponder our sins and consider how Jesus suffered and died for us. We should die for what we've done, but instead we live because he has removed the rod of punishment from us. Therefore we cry boldly to you to comfort us in our sorrows, cleanse us from our sins, and lift us from the ashes. We ask this, confident that Jesus himself will argue our case for us. Be with us for his sake. Amen.

9. HELP ME SEE PAST THIS LIFE

(*Job is speaking.*) "I know that my Redeemer lives, and that in the end he will stand upon the earth." (Job 19:25)

Let's begin with some reflection.

Take a moment to be serious minded. Turn your thoughts to life as you see it going on about you and in your own experience. See whether you don't agree with the man whose name was Job and with many others who say, "Life is an empty hole."

Please, don't be amused by that. This is deadly serious. At some point we have to stop ourselves in the play-acting we call living and ask ourselves, "What is really happening?"

Think! Why is a preponderance of great world literature through the ages based on tragedy? Why does Job's friend Eliphaz say that "man is born to trouble as surely as sparks fly upward"? Why does the Teacher of Ecclesiastes say that everything is meaningless, utterly meaningless? (1:2). Why does a teenage girl in our day speak of "drowning in a sea of loneliness" and of thinking only about "death and dying"?

Think! Who are the real winners in a world full of losers? Are there any?

Look around. What do you see? For every new birth

there will be a corresponding death. For every laugh of joy there's a cry of despair. For every hope of peace there's the threat of war. For every word of praise there's a volume of disapproval.

Look around. Do you see some good things? I think you must. But, do you see anything in this life that is always good?

You're a reasonably well-adjusted Christian person, aren't you? Tell me, in this very day, have you complained about anything? Are you tired from hard work or from lack of sleep or anxious about an important decision? Do you have a headache, muscle aches, an upset stomach? Those whom you love, are they all well and satisfied with the way life is treating them? Do you worry about anyone? How about your schooling? Are you getting the grades you expect and covering all the material you should? Do you like everything that's happening to you?

Imagine for a moment, the building you're in right now — your home, perhaps, or a dormitory — suddenly collapsing and crashing in a heap around you even as you sit there. No, that is unimaginable, isn't it? Still, that very thing has happened to others, it seems with increasing frequency. Earthquakes, volcanoes, hurricanes, floods! I am reminded of the scene in Popayan, Colombia one Sunday. Hundreds of people had gathered in a huge cathedral for worship. Suddenly an earthquake struck. By the time the dust had cleared, you could see the heavens where once the roof covered the cathedral, and at least 40 of the people lay crushed to death where they had been worshiping. At least five other churches collapsed in the quake which killed as many as 300 people. Other disasters, of course, have been even far more devastating. And usually the greatest hurt happens to the friends and family left behind to deal with the tragedy.

It's not right. It's not fair. It's life.

Life is a video game. No matter how well you play, if the alien spacecraft don't get you, the asteroids will. It's only a matter of time.

If we could talk today with the man whose name was Job, he would likely agree. He saw it all and he didn't deserve any of his many troubles — not like you and me. Job can tell us what a rotten deal we get out of life. Just listen, Job is about to speak. He is still sitting there in the ashes. You can't bear to look at his disease-ravaged body. He's going to tell us something about how life really is. Listen to his words.

He says, "I know that my Redeemer lives!"

Dear God of grace and mercy, wherever we look around us we see troubles and suffering. We look at this earthy life and we see signs and threats of death. Teach us, O Lord, to look away from this earth and beyond this life to our living Redeemer and fill our lives with divine meaning. For Jesus' sake. Amen.

10. HELP ME SEE THE LIVING JESUS

(Job is speaking.) **"I know that my Redeemer lives, and that in the end he will stand upon the earth. And after my skin has been destroyed, yet in my flesh I will see God; I myself will see him with my own eyes — I, and not another. How my heart yearns within me!"** **(Job 19:25-27)**

One day as we were nearing the Easter season, my wife saw a little boy looking at her in a store. Attempting to be friendly, she smiled at the boy and said, "Are you looking forward to Easter?" Before the boy could reply, his mother snapped back sharply, "*We* don't celebrate Easter."

That came as something of a shock in our small, heavily-churched town; but it should be no surprise that such an attitude exists around us. Less than half of the population in this country celebrates Easter, and worldwide the percentage is even smaller. The resurrection of Jesus has not made much impact on a large number of people.

They don't believe, not just because they can't accept that a man rose bodily after dying, but also because they have not seen him alive. They have not seen clear evidence that he is alive. You might well expect to hear one of them challenge, "So what if Jesus is alive? What has he done for me lately?"

Well now, if others cannot see Jesus and what he has done lately, who's to blame? A little bit of soul-searching ought to convince us that we may have something to do with it. For example, when I tell someone, "I *know* that my Redeemer lives," do I also live as if I know it? Does it show that I know it? Can someone else clearly see that Jesus is doing something for me?

Who will deny that we ought to derive more comfort, reflect more happiness, find more power, and do more Christlike things than we do — since our Redeemer lives? That's true, and each of us needs to deal with it in his or her life of faith. But it goes much further than that. It goes to a sure hope of life after death. And that is where many stumble.

In fact, the new wave in Christianity — well, actually, just another ripple in the sea of human misunderstanding — warns us we can't be content any longer to look to a life beyond death. The word is: "Make a better world now. Eternity is too far away." To the contrary, my friend, eternity is too close at hand not to look ahead to it. We cannot be content not to look to a life beyond death. If ever Jesus helps us only in this life, then Jesus has failed us. Then he has died for nothing, and Christianity is no better than any other religion or philosophy. No, Jesus died for a purpose — to win our forgiveness and to open heaven for us eternally.

The greater hope we have is illustrated in the story of a blind Hindu boy (born Hindu) who died young. By God's grace, he learned many important Bible passages at the feet of a missionary. In the hour that death stalked him, he exulted, "I know that my Redeemer lives." And again and again, while his voice was failing, he cried, "I know, I know!" And at the last moment, "I see, I see, I see a great light! I see him in his beauty! Tell my teacher that the blind boy sees! Glory, glory!" Those were his last words.

When Job spoke the words that inspired that boy's cry of faith in the face of death, Job, too, had no more hope for life on earth. He felt his life was coming to an end, and he even begged that the end might come quickly.

Standing as it were on the edge of his grave, Job looked up from the black hole before him and looked beyond it to the very end of time. He saw his Redeemer, who is also your Redeemer and my Redeemer, alive and standing upon the earth. And he realized — as surely as Jesus later said, "Because I live, you also will live" (John 14:19) — that he (Job) would stand too to see his God long after the grave would have decayed his body. "I myself will see him with my own eyes —" he said, "I, and not another. How my heart yearns within me!"

Take that with you today — the greater hope. Because you know Jesus lives, you also can say, although the grave will threaten to swallow you up forever, "I myself will see him with my own eyes — I, and not another." Say it, and let your heart yearn for it within you, and reflect it to others — because Jesus lives.

Fill our hearts, O God, with the faith and comfort that come from knowing that Jesus, our Redeemer, lives.

28

And lead us in faith safely through death and the grave
to stand with Jesus at the last in eternal glory, through
the Lord Jesus. Amen.

11. HELP ME LET GOD BE GOD

**Then the LORD answered Job out of the storm. He
said: "Who is this that darkens my counsel with
words without knowledge? Brace yourself like a man;
I will question you, and you shall answer me. Where
were you when I laid the earth's foundation? Tell me, if
you understand."**

(Again the LORD is speaking to Job.) **"Brace yourself
like a man; I will question you, and you shall answer
me. Would you discredit my justice? Would you
condemn me to justify yourself? Do you have an arm
like God's, and can your voice thunder like his? Then
adorn yourself with glory and splendor, and clothe
yourself in honor and majesty."**

(Job is replying.) **"Surely I spoke of things I did not
understand, things too wonderful for me to know . . .
My ears had heard of you but now my eyes have seen
you. Therefore I despise myself and repent in dust and
ashes."**

**The LORD blessed the latter part of Job's life more
than the first. (Job 38:1-4; 40, 7-10; 42:3,5,6,12)**

The patience of Job. All over the world people know
about and admire the patience of Job. Christians and Jews
and others as well hold up Job as an example worth
following. Frankly, at the outset of this series on Job I
wondered where we might go, once we had fully discussed
Job's perseverance in his suffering.

Yes, Job emerges front and center in the book that bears his name. And we who know him echo the commonly expressed sentiment, "Oh, for the patience of Job!"

But that's not the end of the matter. We have also seen Job waver and complain and challenge God. We have seen a man, yes, a strong and pious man — nonetheless, one with failings common to human nature. Furthermore, if Job stands large here, it only means that God stands larger. For, in the end, we don't have so much a story about Job as we have a message about God.

Simply put, we learn from Job to let God be God.

But of course! What else? We might as well say, "Let a stone be a stone, a horse be a horse, a rose be a rose." Yes, in a sense. The trouble is that ever since God made man in his own image and, then, man lost that image in sin, man has been trying to make God over in man's own image. We human beings do it again and again. Job did it. He wanted to make God think like him, because in Job's mind God could not have a good reason to make Job suffer as he did. And Job said so.

That's why God accused Job of speaking without knowledge and challenged him with the question, "Where were you when I laid the earth's foundation?"

Except that it's such a tragedy, we might laugh at the way some men try to remake God. The early Greeks, for example, came up with gods and goddesses, more human than divine, gods who slept, felt pain, tricked one another, made fun of one another, felt jealous, and toyed with human beings. Even now some make up a god who could not create the world as God said he did; others, a god who really is many gods and any god; others, a god who merely shows us how to live and grades us A+ for sincere effort.

I suppose it's hard to see that we do the same sort of thing; but we do, simply because, like Job, we expect God to think like us. So we find ourselves justifying our lives before him as if he could and should never be disappointed in us. We question his wisdom in letting certain tragedies happen. We expect him to like us so well he will merely wink at our shortcomings. We try to make God be what we want him to be. So we need the reminder to let God be God.

31

We need the reminder, too, because we need what comes when we see God as God:

1) It humbles us. When you know who God is, then you know who you are next to God. You have nothing to boast about. You have nothing to say. You must confess as Job did, "I despise myself."

2) It directs us to learn from God so that we don't add to his teachings as Job's friends did and so we don't speak foolishly as Job did. Job admitted, "Surely I spoke of things I did not understand."

3) It works repentance. Job again, "I . . . repent in dust and ashes."

4) It calls for trust that God will do what is best. It depends upon God to save because it knows only he can save and because the God of heaven gave his own Son to save, namely, Jesus Christ the ascended Lord.

5) When we let God be God, we experience God's blessings. Look at the amazing outcome for Job: "The Lord blessed the latter part of Job's life more than the first." Yes, the Lord richly blesses us in this life if we let him have his way with us. But the greater blessings will be ours when we join the ascended Savior in his heavenly glory.

The latter part of our life, the part in eternity, will be "blessed more than the first."

Therefore, let God be God.

God of heaven and Savior of the nations, praise be to you, for yours is the kingdom and the power and the glory, forever. Amen.

Series Two
Lord, I'm Calling

12. I WISH . . .

If you remain in me and my words remain in you, ask whatever you wish, and it will be given you. (John 15:7)

> Star light, star bright,
> First star I see tonight,
> Wish I may, wish I might
> Have the wish I wish tonight.

Do you remember that little ritual from your childhood as I do from mine? That bit of childish idolatry (along with making a wish before blowing out birthday candles or breaking the wishbone from Sunday's chicken dinner) has survived for generations apparently because from earliest youth we all have an inherent desire to be able to say, "I wish . . .," and have that wish come true. Of course, most of us really didn't put so much stock in the first star of the night as to expect an answer, but we went through the ritual, just in case. And most of us, I suppose, have not stopped making wishes just because we've left our childhood behind.

I wish, in fact, that I could be granted the traditional three wishes we so often hear about in stories. But so much for the world of pretend. Why would any of us wish on a star or be content with a mere three wishes when we have something much better? That's right, better! Our Lord has promised, unequivocally, "Ask whatever you wish, and it will be given you."

"Whatever you wish . . ." I'm amazed at how much God promises. We're not talking about a childhood ritual now. We're talking about taking God at his word. Still, strangely enough, we often treat prayer to God with little more confidence than wishing on a star. We really don't expect our prayer to come true. We pray with half a heart or as an afterthought. Our prayer life betrays a weakness in our faith life.

I suppose that happens because, what our Savior promises unequivocally he does not offer unconditionally. Jesus says you will get your wishes "if you remain in me and my words remain in you." Therefore, as surely as our faith in Jesus has weaknesses because of our sinful natures, so surely we'll fail to gain all that we can through prayer. Just as surely, whatever we ask out of faith in Jesus, based on his words and promises, we shall receive. Without Jesus and his word, we ask in vain. With Jesus we cannot ask too much from our God.

I know that has held true in my life. For all of my earthly doubts and misgivings, nothing important to me has ever happened without prayer, and many blessings have come which I had no right to expect. God has not always given at the time I thought was opportune; he has just always given at the opportune time. And whatever else I thought I needed first, he has always filled my first needs first in Christ. I pray because Jesus is with me, and he answers for the same reason.

Do you know what I mean? You will if you try it. Think of it, God has given you his own Son for your salvation. "How will he not also, along with him, graciously give us all things?" (Romans 8:32). Jesus is the key. You don't pray because you need Jesus; you pray because you have Jesus. In him and by his word all things worth having belong to you. Just ask. "Ask and it will be given to you" (Luke 11:9). Make a wish in Jesus and it will come true.

Dear God in heaven, I wish that you would open my heart and mouth ever wider to ask you in faith for all good things. I wish that you would help me see ever more clearly that you fulfill all my wishes for Jesus' sake. O Lord, hear my wishes because of Jesus. Amen.

13. I PRAY ACCORDING TO GOD'S WILL

This is the confidence we have in approaching God: that if we ask anything according to his will, he hears us. (1 John 5:14)

God wants you and me to call to him in every need. "Ask whatever you wish," he offers, "and it will be given you." God's Word is clear and his goodness unlimited. "Pray," he says. "Pray, and I will listen."

In response, we have entitled this series of devotions, "Lord, I'm Calling."

Prayer is God's way of letting us make wishes and have them come true. Prayer brings us face to face with God to tell him our needs. "Come boldly," he invites. "Come confidently. Come in faith. I will listen and answer."

Of course, God doesn't just hold out a grab bag of blessings that absolutely anyone can reach into with prayer. You have to be a Christian in order to pray and be heard by God. You have to believe in Jesus. Furthermore, today the Lord tells us that you can have anything you want as long as you ask "according to his will."

I guess, if I were an unbeliever and a cynic, I'd scoff at that condition. And if I didn't think very clearly, I'd probably think like the cynic even though I'm a believer. It's like asking your boss for a raise. If he wants you to have it, he'll give it, otherwise not. So what is God really offering when he promises you anything you ask "according to his will"?

I speak foolishly. "What, indeed!" We're not dealing here with some human employer who will grant our request based upon what he thinks of our performance, upon what good he will gain by giving, upon his own whim or fancy or capriciousness or possibly on what he had for breakfast. We're dealing with God, who already has given us our most precious possession without our deserving, without any performance rating, even without our asking — dealing with God, who has given us the Savior and the faith to believe in him.

Look at what it means to ask "according to his will."

38

His will, foremost, is to keep us on the way of salvation in Christ.

His will operates with perfect wisdom, infinitely wiser than ours.

His will is supreme and he applies it for the well-being of the universe.

His will looks out only for our greatest good. The good God can do no differently.

When you come face to face with God in true prayer, you come trusting in his good and holy will.

To help illustrate: I think first of a somewhat frivolous example, but it helps to make the point. Have you ever wondered what God does with the prayers offered at the free throw lane in a basketball game? The shooter prays he'll make the shot. The opposing center looking for the rebound prays he'll miss it. No, God won't automatically dismiss the prayers — if they are offered in true faith according to his will. But he'll give the "yes" answer just that way — "according to his will." So the Lord must act for the greater good of all whenever true Christians line up in prayer on opposite sides of an issue — say in war, for example.

Or think of how a parent responds to a child who asks for many things. A responsible and loving parent gives only the things that he considers good for the child and keeps harmful things away, even though the child may want them most sincerely. The responsible parent gives the child what is good for his age and situation. The new car, for example, might be a good thing — later.

Or, finally, listen to the prayer of an unknown old Civil

War soldier as he summarized the exercise of God's will in his life:

"I asked God for strength, that I might achieve,
  I was made weak, that I might learn humbly to obey . . . .
I asked for health, that I might do greater things.
  I was given infirmity, that I might do better things . . . .
I asked for riches, that I might be happy,
  I was given poverty, that I might be wise . . . .
I asked for power, that I might have the praise of men,
  I was given weakness, that I might feel the need of God . . . .
I asked for all things, that I might enjoy life,
  I was given life, that I might enjoy all things . . . .
I got nothing that I asked for, but everything I had hoped for.

Almost despite myself, my unspoken prayers were answered. I am among all men, most richly blessed."

In that spirit, according to his will, may your theme be "Lord, I'm Calling."

O God, our God, work in us by the gospel to make our wills completely consistent with yours. Forgive us when we ignore your will, keep us safe from the forces opposed to your will, and help us to realize that your will is always best for us. We pray because it is your will, for Jesus' sake. Amen.

14. I PRAY IN PRIVATE

When you pray, do not be like the hypocrites, for they love to pray standing in the synagogues and on the street corners to be seen by men. I tell you the truth, they have received their reward in full. But when you pray, go into your room, close the door and

pray to your Father, who is unseen. Then your Father, who sees what is done in secret, will reward you." (Matthew 6:5, 6)

40

While I was sitting in a restaurant one day waiting for my meal to come, the two families at the table across the room received theirs. Before starting to eat, they all bowed their heads and one of the men started praying aloud, obviously choosing his words as he prayed. I couldn't miss seeing them pray and hearing them. Nor could I miss it later when one of their children, while being unruly, accidentally smashed a glass.

"Nothing out of the ordinary," you say?

Maybe not. But when the families simply ignored the smashed glass — made no move to pick up any of it, did not attempt to inform a waitress, and failed to reprimand the child even mildly — I couldn't help but observe how totally inconsistent the later scene appeared in contrast with the opening show of piety. Yes, I wondered to myself, "Did they pray more to be seen praying or more because their saving faith moved them to pray?"

I don't know the answer, mind you. And, yes, I too prayed in that restaurant that evening and may also have done something inconsistent with my faith. But, the question remains, more simply put, "Why did they pray so openly? Was it a proper testimony or an improper show?"

Whatever conclusion one draws, just asking the question highlights Jesus' message to us today: "When you pray, go into your room, close the door and pray to your Father, who is unseen." Why be so private about your prayers? Because "the hypocrites" (as Jesus identifies them) love to pray out in public "to be seen by men." In other words, "Don't pray for show."

Please notice, the message is not meant for those already identified as the hypocrites, possibly the family who made the show in the restaurant. It's meant for you and me as we live our lives for Jesus. Jesus emphasizes, "But *you,* whenever you pray," don't be like the hypocrites. Don't set yourself up to be seen as someone who prays. Don't let people — their presence, their opinions — influence your prayer life. And don't make any personal judgments about your schoolmates or others just because they don't show (they're not supposed to) a private prayer life.

I'm struck by a scene that recurs at intervals in school cafeterias when our Lutheran young people eat together. Several persons converge on a table with their trays. As the individuals get settled, several quite automatically say a silent table prayer. Suddenly, one person who has already begun to eat sees that the others are praying. He or she abruptly stops eating and apparently breathes a hurried prayer. Why, I ask, does that person pray — out of faith or out of embarrassment? "What will the others think of me?"

Pray in private. Pray in your room alone with God. Jesus does not make an exclusive statement here about the only place to pray. Rather he reveals an ideal setting in which you can avoid the error of the hypocrites and get the most out of prayer. For when you follow the Lord's advice, you are not even tempted to pray to be seen of people. Others don't know you are praying. You set yourself free from external distractions. You focus your thoughts on the God who has made you his child through Jesus.

Picture it. In private, unseen by anyone but God, you review your own helplessness, yes, and hopelessness. You realize again how alone you are without God. You visualize your Savior, Jesus, as he died alone on the cross so that you might find God in your private room. You come in the name of the living, ascended Savior and speak person to person with the Father in heaven, your Father. And he who sees and hears where all is dark and silent listens and responds.

Go, my friend, at your next opportunity, shut yourself up in a private place and say, "Father, I'm calling."

42

Father in heaven, keep us from the error of the hypocrites. Let us not pray so that others may see us. Rather stir up our hearts by your Spirit to seek you in private, where we can pour out our troubled hearts, knowing that you are listening. Show us the way to you in prayer through Jesus, who is the Way to you in faith. Amen.

IMMANUEL EV. LUTH.
Church Library
Willmar, MN

15. I PRAY WITH OTHERS

"Again, I tell you that if two of you on earth agree about anything you ask for, it will be done for you by my Father in heaven. For where two or three come together in my name, there am I with them." (Matthew 18:19, 20)

"What is private about public prayer?" Someone might feel inclined to ask such a question after hearing Jesus' admonition in our last devotion and placing it next to his words today. "Pray in private," he said, "in your room, alone, with the door closed." Today he says, "Find another or others to pray with."

Actually the two thoughts are entirely compatible with one another, the one seeming to grow out of the other or to be an enlarged version of it. Once again, notice, the intent is not to be seen of people as you pray, it's to join with people in prayer — united in faith and agreed in purpose.

Jesus is not enjoining public prayer of the kind advocated for public schools or invoked at the sporting events of some private schools. He is promoting prayer such as we unite in at worship in our churches and in our campus chapels. He is calling for us to pray together who are united in faith and agreed in purpose.

We come together in our church worship in the name of Jesus Christ our Savior. We come united in faith, intent on continuing in all the ways of Jesus, as he would have it. We come agreed that life's first purpose is to seek and to promote the kingdom of God. We are one in faith and one in spirit. Our hearts beat as one in Christ Jesus our Lord. Our prayers rise as one to heaven's throne. The church's sanctuary is our private room, our house of prayer.

Jesus is with us in church. Oh, of course, he is everywhere, the omnipresent God. But he is there in a special way, as he promised: "Where two or three come together in my name, there am I with them." Jesus is there in his grace, his boundless love, which prompted the very Son of God to sacrifice himself for our salvation. Jesus is there to bring blessings. He is there to assure us that our prayers will reach the God of all creation. Jesus joins our worship to see that we receive all that we need.

We pray in Jesus' name with our hearts bound in faith and in Christian love. And whether one person leads the prayer or all speak the same prayer together, the prayer of many believers fairly shouts to heaven. Not that we prevail upon God with our numbers. We prevail with our faith in his promises which say, ". . . if two of you on earth agree on anything you ask for, it will be done for you by my Father in heaven."

What a powerful, moving thing is the combined prayer of Christians united in faith and agreed in purpose. Luther agreed: "Combined prayer is precious," he said, "and the most effective." You certainly wouldn't have gotten any argument from the Apostle Peter. At the time that Herod (after he'd had James the brother of John put to death with the sword) seized Peter and threw him into prison, we learn that "the church was earnestly praying to God for him" (Acts 12:5). You know how God answered the prayer. Peter walked away free from chains and prison, past guards, accompanied by an angel.

44   God hears our combined prayers. Do we appreciate that? Do we pray the more earnestly because we know it? Or do we treat lightly such an essential part of our worship as prayer? Let us remember, when we gather together in one faith, Jesus is with us, and let us pray together earnestly and confidently.

O Lord, cause us to cherish the unity of faith and agreement in purpose we enjoy in our churches. Lead us to make the most of the opportunities you provide for us to pray together. Keep us strong in our faith and comforted by your presence, for Jesus' sake. Amen.

16. I PRAY NONSTOP

Pray continually. (1 Thessalonians 5:17)

Do you pray without stopping? Do you even pray once every ten minutes without fail? Once every hour?

Do you even *care* to pray so often? I know that as a Christian and a pastor I sometimes feel a need to assure people that good Christians do not necessarily go around with their hands folded in constant prayer.

But now I call your attention to God's word as it says unmistakably, "Pray continually." And in case you wonder about the word "continually," it means in the original language literally "without any gaps or intervals." God wants nonstop prayer.

So now what are we to think — we who are quick to admit, even proud to say, we don't pray all the time?

In this light, I see two sides to God's word here in answer to us. I see a warning and I see a wonder.

God would warn us here about our attitude toward prayer. Let us not pray sparingly, and be glad we do, when God says, "Pray continually." Let us not grow cool to nonstop prayer, prayer that continues, prayer that perseveres.

This is a warning about attitude. For when we don't care to pray continually, we become dangerously like the farmer who, when asked whether or not he ever prayed, replied, "To be on the safe side, I do a little praying now and then. The way I figure, it can't do me any harm."

"I do a little praying now and then . . . to be on the safe side." How *safe* do you suppose that is?

Where in such prayer is the faith — that warm, living contact with Christ the Savior? Where is the realization that God's Son has opened a free line of communication between us and the Father in heaven? Where is the confidence that Jesus meant it when he told us to try prayer and promised that it would work?

Did you ever see a child with a brand new walkie-talkie — I mean one that really works, that transmits clearly for half a block or more? He'll use that walkie-talkie over and over again talking with his unseen friend. Well, we have a walkie-talkie that connects us to the unseen God. Who of us will say that he or she doesn't care to use it, constantly?

In spite of what was said earlier, I trust that none of us wants to say that. I'm sure also that none of us means to downgrade nonstop prayer, even though we still feel we do not want to join a parade of human praying mantises who must fold hands and chant our ways to and from our daily tasks.

But that brings us to the wonder of it. For even when our

attitude favors continuous prayer, it is a wonder that we can do it. It is a wonder of faith and of the love of God.

To realize the wonder we first need to realize that prayer is not just the words we say or the way we hold our hands; it is communion with God.

Perhaps we can illustrate with the example of the young aviation cadet who, when asked what he did before his first solo flight, replied, "I prayed, 'Not my will but thine be done.'"

"But," someone questioned, "how did you expect that to help you?"

"Just by putting me in tune with God," he answered.

That can be a way of describing nonstop prayer, namely, going through your days "in tune with God." Paul comments on this matter when he says to the Ephesians, "And pray in the spirit on all occasions with all kinds of prayers and requests" (6:18).

"Pray in the spirit." I believe you can take that word "spirit" with a small *s* or a capital *S* because it has to involve both. For when God's Spirit is at work in your spirit, he puts you in tune with God. In your spirit you keep God close to you, draw on him for help and comfort in all things, yes, pray to him. That's just one more of the many wonders of trust in Jesus Christ as your Savior, the wonder of nonstop prayer. Use it.

Dear God, loving Father, keep us in tune with you so that we can commune with you in all things. Strengthen our faith by your Spirit for the sake of your Son and be ever ready to answer our prayers as they come continually to your throne. In Jesus' name. Amen.

17. I PRAY WITHOUT "MANY WORDS"

"When you pray, do not keep on babbling like pagans, for they think they will be heard because of their many words."(Matthew 6:7)

Have you engaged in nonstop prayer since reading the last devotion? As surely as Jesus is your Savior, you have gained if you did. You are in tune with God.

On the other hand, if you went into your room last night and prayed the Lord's Prayer 100 times before falling asleep, you probably didn't gain anything at all.

Do you see the important difference?

Yesterday God could say to us, "Pray continually." Today he can warn us against praying so as to be heard because of our "many words." And he can say these things without contradiction, because the very reason we can profit from continuous prayer is the reason we cannot profit from merely repeating a host of prayer words. It's the spirit of the matter — God's Spirit at work in our spirit, keeping us in communion with him.

True prayer issues not from the lips but from the heart, the heart lifted up by faith in Jesus. As Luther said it, prayers issued without the heart also rising to God are "prayers as much as scarecrows in the garden are men. The essence is not there, but only the appearance and the name." So beware of praying the way the heathen do, mouthing prayer words just because it is the custom and is expected. Beware of simply repeating formulaic prayers — yes, even the Lord's Prayer — as if the formula by itself has some kind of magic with God and especially so if we repeat it often.

With this same kind of understanding, Luther, who once admonished us Christians to be "incessant and constant" in our praying, also claimed, "The fewer the words, the better the prayer." "Few words and much meaning is Christian," he insisted. "Many words and little meaning is heathenish."

But the Lord does not tell us we must never pray long prayers. Jesus' prayer recorded in John 17 fills the whole chapter of 26 verses and takes several minutes to pray. Nor does he say we should simply not repeat prayers. Jesus did that in the Garden of Gethsemane. And, of course, if a prescribed prayer were wrong, he wouldn't have prescribed a prayer for us to use.

Where does this leave you in your prayer life? Do you wonder sometimes whether you pray often enough, whether your prayers are long enough, whether they have enough meaning, whether you have repeated too much or too little?

I can't give you the answers to such questions, but I can tell you where to find the answers. Go to the cross of Jesus. Recount all that cross means for you. There the God of mercy and grace fulfilled all his promises to make an open pathway to him in heaven. On the cross God sacrificed his own Son as the payment necessary for the countless sins that plague our lives and threaten our destruction. There God reached out through his Son to receive you as his own child. Go to the cross and remember that Jesus, who died there, rose again and will come again to take you to himself. And the living Jesus tells you to pray.

When you go to the cross, your faith will grow. And when your faith grows, your prayer life improves. You pray the right way guided by your faith.

> O thou by whom we come to God,
>   The Life, the Truth, the Way,
> The path of prayer thyself hast trod, —
>   Lord, teach us how to pray. Amen.

18. I CAN'T FIND THE WORDS TO PRAY

In the same way, the Spirit helps us in our weakness. We do not know what we ought to pray, but the Spirit himself intercedes for us with groans that words cannot express. And he who searches our hearts knows the mind of the Spirit, because the Spirit intercedes for the saints in accordance with God's will. (Romans 8:26, 27)

This message does not belong to the strong among us. It speaks to the weak. It holds nothing for the self-confident. It touches only those who find no hope in themselves. The words do not address the self-content. They reach out to those who groan inwardly and wait eagerly. God's Word here talks to me; it talks to you.

Allow me to illustrate: I believe in Jesus Christ. I am —this very letter in this same chapter assures me — I am a child of God. I am not condemned though sin assails me from the inside and from the outside. I have a hope, the hope that belongs to those who are God's children in Jesus Christ. I eagerly await the fulness of that hope, the glory to come in heaven with Jesus. Nevertheless, I sometimes groan inwardly because the wait is hard.

Meanwhile, I am also weak, oh so weak. I face and feel sufferings like everyone around me, like you. Maybe you hurt on the outside and I on the inside, but we both hurt. Maybe my problems are small next to your problems, but we both have problems. Maybe I appear strong while you feel weak, but we are both weak.

Now comes the clincher. I have what is right from God, but I experience what is wrong in me and in this world. I need help from God to keep going. I need to call to him to lead me through the darkness that prevails before the glory to come. I thirst for some relief from the present sufferings. I sigh a deep sigh, but *I cannot find the words to say to God.*

Are you with me? You're suffering. God only knows how much and in what way. So you try to pray. But you don't know what to say. You don't even know what the suffering might possibly mean or what you truly need to relieve it. You cannot find the words to speak to God, and the spirit in you groans and sighs under the burden.

Don't despair. God hears you and me.

What? He hears us when we don't even know what we are saying?

That's right, he hears. He understands. He knows exactly the words we want to say because, when we don't know how to pray, the Holy Spirit prays for us. The Spirit of God turns our groans into exactly what we ought to say to God in accordance with his own will.

God does not leave us alone, ever. He takes care of our every need. He hears our every cry. His Spirit speaks for us from the depths of our being. His Son speaks for us at his throne on high. And we live in his loving care.

O God, my God, though in this very moment I bring only a collection of deep-felt groans and sighs for my prayer, I know you are listening in detail to all that I need, as your Spirit intercedes for me. In that way, too, hear me. O Lord, I'm calling. For Jesus' sake. Amen.

19. I TAKE TIME OUT TO PRAY

Jesus often withdrew to lonely places and prayed. (Luke 5:16)

How is your prayer life?

We have been exploring God's promises about prayer under the theme, "Lord, I'm Calling." We've heard we can call to God directly for anything we wish according to his will. We have received encouragement to pray privately as well as to share praying with our fellow believers in public worship. We have heard about the possibility of nonstop prayer while avoiding meaningless repetition. We have even seen that God's Holy Spirit will voice prayers for us when we cannot find the words.

So, how is it going?

Let me ask the question a different way: "Do you take time out to pray?" Everything we have said about prayer is only academic unless we take time to do it.

In this text, we don't have an exhortation to take time out to pray; we have an example. Just look whose example we have: "Jesus often withdrew to lonely places and prayed." Jesus prayed with regularity. He who taught us to pray, himself prayed. He who answers prayer, himself prayed. He whose name gives power to prayer, himself prayed. He had no guilt to confess, no mercy to implore, no cleansing to seek; but still he prayed. Our sinless Savior, our perfect Substitute, our God yet man, spoke to his heavenly Father in prayer. He took time out, went away alone and prayed.

Many wonder what Jesus said in his several prayers. Actually, it's not difficult to piece some of that together, since a few of Jesus' prayers are recorded. He asked for support in his human nature for the work he had to do. He expressed love and thankfulness to his Father. He prayed for the souls of sinful people. There's more, but for now let us simply marvel that he often went off alone to pray.

Let us marvel and ask ourselves, "If Jesus took time out to pray, how much more should we?" He was pure. We are guilty. Who needs the more to pray? He was strong. We are weak. Who needs the more to pray? He was wise. We are foolish. Who needs the more to pray? He gave up his perfect, divine life for us. Let us take time out to pray.

We have every reason to pray, but we must struggle to set aside the time. As Luther said it, "When I would speak and pray to God by myself, a hundred thousand hindrances at once intervene before I get at it." The devil, Luther would remind us, is a master at turning our thoughts away from prayer. "I still find it necessary," Luther underscored, "every day to look for time during which I may offer prayer."

That's the challenge today's text leaves with us: look for time to offer prayer. Make time; seize opportunities. Let the man of faith in you overpower the old man of the flesh, and take time to talk to God. Start at the most obvious times, such as each time you prepare for worship. Begin your day, just before you roll out of bed, with a prayer. Never start or finish a meal without prayer. Pick at least one time during each day to be alone in prayer. And don't let sleep close your eyes at night until you have prayed.

Improve your prayer life, and improve your life.

Dear God, our Father in heaven, we count among our faults the neglect of prayer, the frequent failure to talk to you as you have invited us to do through your Son, Jesus Christ. For his sake forgive us also this sin and give us strength to set aside time regularly for prayer. Let us learn from Jesus' example and improve our lives through prayer. In his name we ask it. Amen.

20. I PRAY FOR EVERYONE

I urge, then, first of all, that requests, prayers, intercession and thanksgiving be made for everyone." (1 Timothy 2:1)

Back in the late sixties and early seventies in the face of mounting troubles everywhere, the cry went up loud and clear: "God is dead." Of course, mostly those who didn't believe in God in the first place and those who didn't understand his salvation were saying it.

Then, as the Christian community began to respond to that latest attack on faith, a bumper sticker appeared which read, "God isn't dead. I just talked with him this morning."

Although the particular controversy that gave rise to that bumper sticker has since grown into other shapes and taken on other appearances, the double-barrelled miracle in the bumper sticker message still blasts through the false images. God the Son died, to be sure, but he rose again and ascended into heaven, and he lives eternally together with God the Father and God the Holy Spirit. God lives, guiding the courses of individuals and of nations toward the Great Day at the end of time when Jesus will return to judge all people. Meanwhile, we can talk with him each day.

We have been focusing on that latter thought in this series of devotions under the theme, "Lord, I'm Calling." And we have found that our living God is listening.

Yes, he's listening, but that leaves us yet with a question: "What are we to say to him?" Oh, it's easy enough to say, "Lord, I want. Lord, I need. Lord, give me." Surely, however, you sense that such one-dimensional, self-centered praying fails to make fullest use of this miracle of talking with God. So we turn now to the word of the Apostle Paul as he gives us some direction for our prayers. He mentions several kinds of prayers we should pray on behalf of everyone.

The first kind of prayer our text calls "requests." Those are the "I need" prayers, except that God wants us to recognize that "I" am not the only one with needs. We need to say our prayers for everyone. And when we do, think of what it means: We'll *see* the needs of others. We'll think less of our own needs. As the old saw puts it, "I used to feel bad because I had no shoes, but then I met a man with no feet." Pray for the man with no feet, and you also will receive help.

The second kind of prayer our text simply calls "prayers." These include the "I need" prayers, but the stress in this word is on a worshipful attitude. It includes giving honor to God, confessing his name, recognizing that his will is best. In this prayer you will ask God to strengthen all believers by his Spirit and to reach all unbelievers with his truth of salvation. With this attitude of prayer you will remember that spiritual blessings will help everyone more than material or physical blessings.

The third kind of prayer our text calls "intercession." This is the "talking-with-God" kind of prayer, and the conversation is usually on behalf of someone else. In such prayers you save your own petitions until you have brought the petitions of others to God's attention. And, when you do so, you exercise Christian love which, Paul says elsewhere, "is not self-seeking" (1 Corinthians 13:5).

At last Paul suggests "thanksgiving" for everyone. Every time you pray, be sure to say, "Thank you, God," in some way. To fail in thankfulness is to overlook the wonder and privilege of prayer itself. It's a failure to see that God for Jesus' sake cares about everyone and answers every prayer brought in true faith.

What, then, should you say when you pray? Say, "God bless Harvey and Fritz and Sally and Sue, Dad and Mom and Grampa too, the President and those in power, the nameless millions with needs this hour."

Say, "God, merciful Lord and Savior, glory to your name, may all the earth shout praise."

Say, "Lord, Jimmy Jones needs you and needs you now. Be with him, Lord, be with him."

Say, "Lord, thank you, for Jesus' sake."

God of mercy and love, praise be to you in all things. Bless, O Lord, all those who seek your blessings in this very hour. Be with my loved ones to make their faith stronger and their lives better. Shed your grace over all the world that people everywhere may learn of it and be saved. With grateful heart and in Jesus' name I pray. Amen.

21. I PRAY THE PERFECT PRAYER

"This, then, is how you should pray: 'Our Father in heaven, hallowed be your name, your kingdom come, your will be done on earth as it is in heaven. Give us today our daily bread. Forgive us our debts, as we also have forgiven our debtors. And lead us not into temptation, but deliver us from evil.'" (Matthew 6:9-13)

What are we to say when we pray? When we addressed that question in the last devotion, perhaps you began to anticipate today's text. As an example of what to say in our prayers there's no prayer like the Lord's Prayer. It is the perfect prayer.

So we can pray this prayer a thousand times and still feel a thrill to pray it the one thousand and first time. We can have a thousand unspeakable problems we want God to hear, and this prayer will cover them all. We can feel we need a thousand things, and this prayer will remind us that we already have what is the most important.

Let's look at just a few of the wonderful blessings the Lord's Prayer provides. I say, "just a few," because to attempt more would demand at least another entire series of messages like this one.

The prayer begins, "Our Father in heaven," and as we say

the words we express faith, love and hope. In fact, the words express our *saving faith* in Jesus, for only by faith in him can we call God our Father and call upon him to treat us as his children. The *love* we express by including all Christians in our petitions — he is *our* Father. When, for example, you next pray this prayer, remember the rest of us (wherever we may be) who have shared these same devotions, because we are included. And we have *hope* because this is our Father "in heaven." In him we learn the true meaning of fatherhood and from him, the Almighty, we receive all that is good.

Pause for a moment. Think of it. Before you make a single request in this perfect prayer, as soon as you have said, "Our Father in heaven," you've prayed all you need to pray in order to know that your requests are heard and answered.

"Hallowed be your name, your kingdom come, your will be done on earth as it is in heaven." Notice how quickly the focus of attention shifts from us to the heavenly Father — to his name, his kingdom, his will. When we are right with God, everything is right with our lives. If everyone were right with God, everything would be right with the world. So we pray to be right, to know his name by his Word and to live by it, to have him rule in our hearts by the Holy Spirit and to reach the hearts of everyone, to have his will prevail among us and to have our own wills in harmony with his. God is all in all. Pray that we might be in him and he in us.

"Give us today our daily bread." Ah, did I speak of wonderful blessings? The Lord Jesus knows we have basic needs for our earthly survival. We can pray for those too, knowing God will provide. So great is his bounty that though we need only bread, he gives meat and potatoes and vegetables and dessert as well.

"Forgive us our debts as we have forgiven our debtors." Call them trespasses, call them sins — we need to be set free from the insurmountable debt we owe to God. And since we have our forgiveness in Jesus Christ, we need to develop a forgiving spirit ourselves, knowing that we are never asked to forgive as much as God has forgiven us. Think of what it means to be able to ask for forgiveness, knowing we have it — each time we ask and even before we ask.

"And lead us not into temptation, but deliver us from evil." We place ourselves into God's hands to guard and keep and guide us in every danger and trial, to carry us over the pits and snares prepared by the devil, until at last we leave all evil behind as we enter God's heaven.

Here our text ends without the familiar doxology, "for yours is the kingdom and the power and the glory forever." It's not there because it shows up only in later manuscripts of the Bible. Never mind that, however, because whenever you pray the Lord's Prayer even with only an imperfect awareness of its perfect petitions, your heart must surely burst with praise at the end. For God's is "the kingdom and the power and the glory forever. Amen." Even if this doxology was not originally located here these words express a scriptural truth. So it is and so shall it be.

> Our Father who art in heaven,
> Hallowed be thy name.
> Thy kingdom come.
> Thy will be done on earth as it is in heaven.
> Give us this day our daily bread.
> And forgive us our trespasses as we forgive those who
>   trespass against us.
> And lead us not into temptation;
> But deliver us from evil.
> For thine is the kingdom and the power and the glory
>   forever and ever. Amen.

Series Three
Lord, I'm on the Way

22. I AM YOUR SERVANT

**Simon Peter, a servant and apostle of Jesus Christ,
To those who through the righteousness of our God
and Savior Jesus Christ have received a faith as
precious as ours:**

**Grace and peace be yours in abundance through
the knowledge of God and of Jesus our Lord. (2 Peter
1:1, 2)**

61

Dear Friend,

Note carefully how I just addressed you. "Dear Friend," I
said. It sounds rather bland and uninteresting, doesn't it? A
quick way to get started and to get on with the message, a
mere formality. Similarly, we begin most of the letters we
write, "Dear So-and-so." It's so routine I wonder why we
even bother to use it.

Actually, the greeting has deep and significant meaning.
When you call someone "dear," you are saying that person
is loved, is precious, is highly esteemed by you. And when I
add the word "Friend," I mean most sincerely that I
consider you a friend in Jesus Christ.

I mention this primarily so that you might see in contrast
all Peter does with the greeting in his letter. I mention it
because I fear many of us tend to read the greeting of a
biblical letter much the same way we read the greeting of a
modern day letter: "Simon Peter . . . mmmm . . . to those . . .
mmmm . . . who have received faith . . . mmmm . . . grace
and peace . . . mmmm . . . Jesus our Lord." Now, on to the
substance. We think of a greeting as a hurdle we have to
pass on our way to, we hope, better things.

What a pity in this case. What a waste!

Far from filling his greeting with inconsequential plati-
tudes, Peter loads it with beneficial meaning. His greeting is
like a letter in itself. Without Peter's greeting, you can hardly

understand the rest of his letter. Without it you are like the person who comes ten minutes late for a movie in which the full plot was set in the first five minutes.

Let's look more closely at what we may have missed. Pay close attention now because this is an apostle writing. That's what he calls himself. This apostle walked with Jesus and learned from Jesus person to person. He was one of three who got closest to Jesus during the Lord's ministry on earth. Yes, Jesus sent this Peter out — thus "apostle," "one sent out" — sent him out with the others to set the foundation in the building of the church. The apostle brings a message straight from Jesus.

Should we then focus our attention on Peter the apostle as a man great in his own right? No, not at all! Just listen to what he says. Before he is an apostle, he is a "servant" of Jesus Christ. Peter writes as a slave doing the bidding of a gracious Master. Although he's still an apostle, he will turn our thoughts to the Master whom he serves.

Already we have quite enough for a full sermon, you know. For we are, like Peter, slaves in the service of Christ. And we need to be thinking of how we can serve.

That's right, you are every bit like Peter. I'm not saying that — he is. You share, he assures you, his most valuable possession. In his words, you "have received a faith as precious as" his own and as that of the rest of the earliest believers in Jesus.

You have a "precious" faith. Do you ever stop to meditate on what a precious thing your faith is? God himself gave it to you. With it you receive every good thing God has to give, especially every spiritual good. In it, you belong to God. By it, you will serve.

You have your faith, in Peter's words, "through the right-eousness of our God and Savior Jesus Christ." Those words hold out the whole of God's gospel to you. Jesus is "our God and Savior." By the way, don't ever let anyone tell you the Bible doesn't identify Jesus as God. This is just one of the places. The rest of what Peter has to say depends on it.

Now this Jesus in his perfect righteousness also as man has worked out our salvation. As man he took our place. As God he made it count. As the righteous man, he died the death we have deserved for our unrighteousness. As God, he conquered death to lead the way to eternal life for us.

63

So we believe. And so we grow in his love, his "grace" and "peace," as Peter says it. We grow the more we learn and have "knowledge of God and of Jesus our Lord." That's the very reason we have Sunday sermons and Bible classes and catechism classes and Christian schools: to help you learn more of God and what he has done for you in Jesus, to help you increase in God's grace and peace, to help you realize your potential as a "servant," a slave, of Jesus.

This does not exhaust the things we can learn from Peter's greeting. It merely exhausts the space we have allotted here for it. But he's given us some things to ponder, namely: Jesus Christ is our God and Savior. We are his servants. We have a precious faith. And by continually learning more of God and of Jesus our Lord we shall increase in his blessings of grace and peace.

There you have it — greetings from Peter, my dear friend.

Dear Lord God, having heard your greetings this day from your Apostle Peter, we ask you now to increase the blessings of grace and peace among us. Help us to learn more of and to know better your Word and Way. Use us in your service for the sake of Jesus, our God and Savior. Amen.

23. I AM RICH AND PRIVILEGED

64

His [Jesus'] divine power has given us everything we need for life and godliness through our knowledge of him who called us by his own glory and goodness. Through these he has given us his very great and precious promises, so that through them you may participate in the divine nature and escape the corruption in the world caused by evil desires. (2 Peter 1:3, 4)

Rich and privileged.

Do you think those words might possibly describe you? Probably not. Maybe Dr. Jones and his family, Banker Smith and his, or Corporate President Reynolds and his, but not you and me. Maybe not, but Peter says we have "everything we need." If you believe him, you have to believe you're rich.

Peter puts it this way: "[The] divine power [of Jesus] has given us everything we need for life and godliness." In other words, we can measure our riches in Jesus. His divine power gives us whatever we need.

In case that sounds a little too magical and conjures up an image of a divine genie granting wishes with the snap of a finger or the wiggle of a nose, you need to know that this power is found in the gospel of Jesus, which the Apostle Paul also calls "the power of God for . . . salvation" (Romans 1:16). Jesus, by his perfect life and undeserved death, by his torturous suffering and glorious resurrection, has exercised a power that gives us "everything we need for life and godliness."

". . . for life." To sustain our lives and bring them along to their fulfilled purpose, Jesus took away the sin which brings death. He created a new life in us by his Spirit and has begun in us the everlasting life that continues in heaven. Yes, "he

who did not spare his own Son, but gave him up for us all"
has graciously given us "all things" (Romans 8:32).

". . . for godliness." Under the influence of Jesus' power,
that is, in the faith in Jesus worked by the Holy Spirit, we live
our lives in reverence and in worshipful obedience to God.
This happens because we know the Lord by his Word and
because, since he called us to faith, we appreciate, yes,
marvel at, his great "glory and goodness" and his "precious
promises."

Rich and privileged.

Already the riches we enjoy from the Lord make us
privileged. Yet Peter shows us another dimension that
makes us privileged indeed. For through his glory and
goodness and by his great promises the Lord Jesus has
provided that "you may participate in the divine nature and
escape the corruption in the world caused by evil desires."

"You may participate in the divine nature."

You anticipate that coming to pass in all its fulness in the
glories of heaven, but it is your privilege right now to the
extent you use what God has given you.

How do you participate in the divine nature? You enjoy
the very presence of Christ in you by his gospel. Draw on his
presence, and you will put aside and "escape the corruption
in the world caused by evil desires." In plain English, you will
flee temptations.

When the invitation comes, for instance, to drink illegally
or, if you are of legal age, to get drunk, you will turn it down.
When your body begins to yearn for immoral sexual
experiences, you will deny your body. When you feel
inclined to steal or cheat or malign the reputation of others
or defy authority, you will turn instead to Jesus who is with
you and, in your faith, escape the evil desires. You can't do
those things on your own, but you have the opportunity to
be helped by participating "in the divine nature."

Now, we must confess that we often don't try very hard to

escape the corruption and evil desires of the world. We squander our riches and abuse our privileges from God, and we do so at our own peril, for we have to face the consequences of the corruption. Still we toy with the very riches that sustain our lives. We test God's longsuffering. We treat Jesus as someone to be let in and out of our lives at our own convenience. We sink dangerously low.

Marvel, then, so much the more that he still gives "everything we need for life and godliness" and that he still invites us to share in his "divine nature." Marvel at the glory and goodness of Jesus Christ, and resolve to make the most of the riches and privileges we enjoy from him.

Dear God almighty, with your power and in your love you have made us rich and privileged. Give us an extra measure of the power of your gospel so that we may make the most of what you have made us. Help us to be more godly and to escape evil desires more effectively with the help and presence of your Son Jesus Christ. In his name. Amen.

24. I STRIVE FOR FRUITS OF FAITH

For this very reason, make every effort to add to your faith goodness; and to goodness, knowledge; and to knowledge, self-control; and to self-control, perseverance; and to perseverance, godliness; and to godliness, brotherly kindness; and to brotherly kindness, love. For if you possess these qualities in increasing measure, they will keep you from being ineffective and unproductive in your knowledge of our Lord Jesus Christ. But if anyone does not have

them, he is nearsighted and blind, and has forgotten that he has been cleansed from his past sins.

Therefore, my brothers, be all the more eager to make your calling and election sure. For if you do these things, you will never fall, and you will receive a rich welcome into the eternal kingdom of our Lord and Savior Jesus Christ. (2 Peter 1:5-11)

In the previous two devotions we shared the greeting and opening words of Peter in his second letter. In his greeting Peter reminded us that Jesus is our God and Savior and that we have a precious faith in Jesus. Then he told us that we are rich and privileged by virtue of all that God has done for us and that we share in the divine nature.

"For this very reason," Peter now continues. He has reminded his reader that God has made them his own in Christ Jesus, that he has given them everything they need for life and godliness, that through faith in Jesus they participate in the divine nature, and now he urges them, "Make every effort to add to your faith goodness . . . knowledge . . . self-control . . . perseverance . . . godliness . . . brotherly kindness . . . love." Try just as hard as your favorite sports team will try to win its next game; strive for all these seven virtues.

Now I have some problems. If we were getting ready to conduct a pep rally, I would ask you to stand up and cheer for the likes of "goodness," "self-control," "godliness," and "love," and you would perhaps stand up and cheer. But God doesn't ask you to cheer for these good qualities; he calls for you to make them part of your life. That, in turn, only compounds my perplexity. What do all these good things mean in my life? Can I put them into a computer and print out all the answers to life's problems? Will they help us win a football game? Will they put food on my table?

Probably not. Yet when you "make every effort," as Peter

says it, your every decision, your every action, your every step will turn in the direction indicated by these virtues.

When, for example, others make fun of what you believe, suggest you can ignore parts of what God says, and, sneering, call for you to join the 20th century, you exercise what the text here calls "goodness" (really a kind of courage in your faith) when you stand your ground.

When you turn down the chance to go out for a good time because you have to study, or when you take an extra fifteen minutes out each day to read God's Word, you are concerned for "knowledge."

When you turn off the sex-filled TV programs and shun the drugs and drinks that promise heavenly highs, you exercise "self-control."

"Perseverance" sticks with God and endures even when it hurts to do so.

"Godliness" brings you to church — not because someone might otherwise catch you skipping, but because you want to be there.

"Brotherly kindness" makes you friends with your fellow Christians even though you have differences hard to understand.

"Love" makes you think more about what other people need than what you yourself need, including other people who might never be your friends.

That begins to suggest what these seven virtues might mean in your life. Peter suggests that without them we become "ineffective and unproductive in . . . [our] knowledge of our Lord Jesus Christ"; we proceed blindly into the future; and we forget that we have been "cleansed from . . . [our] past sins."

On the positive side, when we want the knowledge of our Lord Jesus Christ to count for something, we shall exercise these virtues. When we open our eyes of faith to see beyond the immediate pleasures and riches or setbacks and upsets of this life to the fulness and glory of eternal life, we shall strive to develop these virtues in our lives of faith. When we remember and appreciate how God's own Son sacrificed himself to win forgiveness for the sins we have committed, we shall want to "make every effort" to "possess these qualities in increasing measure."

69

Let your faith so live, and you will not stumble and become lost in your blindness. Rather, you will be making "your calling and election sure," and "you will receive a rich welcome into the eternal kingdom of our Lord and Savior Jesus Christ."

Dear Lord Jesus, never let me forget the forgiveness you've won for my sins nor let me walk blindly in the ways of darkness, but rather strengthen me in my faith and give me the resolve and power to make every effort to live for you. For your name's sake. Amen.

25. I WALK IN THE TRUTH

We did not follow cleverly invented stories when we told you about the power and coming of our Lord Jesus Christ, but we were eyewitnesses of his majesty. For he received honor and glory from God the Father when the voice came to him from the Majestic Glory, saying, "This is my Son, whom I love; with him I am well pleased." We ourselves heard this voice that came from heaven when we were with him on the sacred mountain. (2 Peter 1:16-18)

Let me tell you briefly the stories of two well-known men. The first came into this world little heralded among the people, although the angels sang at his birth. His mother, a virgin made to conceive by the Holy Spirit, bore the child in a stable and placed him into a feeding trough for his first bed.

He lived in relative obscurity while growing to manhood, when suddenly he burst onto the scene of history as a prophet and a miracle worker. He did good things wherever he went, always looking out for the welfare of others. He called upon people to deny themselves, take up their crosses and follow him. When he did not satisfy the people by doing miracles on demand and creating a powerful earthly kingdom, they put him to death on a cross as a common criminal.

But that did not end his story, because he rose again from the dead and ascended into heaven. He has promised, and his closest followers have echoed the promise, that he will come to us again in power and glory. Watch, therefore, and pray because he's coming soon.

The second man also is widely regarded as a miracle worker. He's a roundish man with a long white beard and a twinkle in his eye. He's been credited with distributing gifts to hundreds of thousands of homes in a single night. He, too, looks for followers to live in his spirit, but after his annual day of doing good, he disappears from the scene, little thought of until another year rolls around. He gives, but only to those who deserve it — keeping close watch with an omniscient eye on those who have been bad or good, naughty or nice. "Be good for goodness' sake," because he's coming again at the appointed time this year.

We already know about both of these men and have experienced the spirit of each. Their stories converge each December, and the whole world knows about them. The most learned persons in the world tend to dismiss their stories as cleverly devised myths or fables. For some that means to reject the men with a "Bah, humbug!" For others it means to patronize the fables' followers for the spirit of goodness the stories seem to generate.

70

Religious leaders generally put more stock in the first man because they're quite sure he really lived, but nobody has ever really seen the roundish man in the red suit. The religious leaders tend to agree, however, that both men's stories have been enhanced by make-believe.

People in general line up somewhere close to the religious leaders, although you will usually see them in December making much more of the gift-giver with a twinkle in his eye than of the manger child of Bethlehem — whose way leads to the cross.

How do we regard the stories of these two men? Truth or fiction? Fantasy or fantastic reality? We have no trouble knowing what to make of Santa Claus. We realize that he often fares better among the people just because he is a product of their imagination. And we need to be careful that his "be-good-to-gain-good" message doesn't deceive us into thinking we can be as good as we need to be.

We have no trouble knowing what to make of Jesus either, thanks to the Lord himself and the men like Peter who make him known to us. Peter assures us that we can trust in Jesus. "We did not follow cleverly invented stories," Peter emphasizes, "when we told you about the power and coming of our Lord Jesus Christ."

The idea that the truth of Jesus is a myth, you see, did not just surface in the intellect of enlightened modern society. Peter faced it and countered it. "We were eyewitnesses of his majesty," he continues, and we might call them "ear-witnesses" as well. Peter, James and John saw the Child of the stable and the Man of the cross as the God of glory on the Mount of Transfiguration. They heard the voice of the Father in heaven declare, "This is my Son, whom I love; with him I am well pleased." The Father was pleased because Jesus humbled himself and was perfectly obedient to the Father's will even though that obedience finally required his sacrificial death on the cross. That sacrifice atoned for the sins of the world and purchased salvation for us all.

Watch and pray! Santa Claus will never come to town and satisfy all our needs and desires, but Jesus will come again in power and glory to receive us into his heavenly home.

> Dear God of glory, through eyewitnesses you have revealed to us your Son as the Babe of Bethlehem, as the Savior at the cross and as the King of heaven. Help us to praise him properly on his birthday, to receive him humbly in his grace, and to look for him to come again in glory, for his name's sake. Amen.

26. I FOLLOW THE LIGHT OF YOUR WORD

We have the word of the prophets made more certain, and you will do well to pay attention to it, as to a light shining in a dark place, until the day dawns and the morning star rises in your hearts. (2 Peter 1:19)

Each year about Christmas time, the Crystal Cathedral in California, made famous by the radio and television ministry of Dr. Robert Schuller, features a grand pageant called "The Glory of Christmas." For a designated donation, you can see live camels, a donkey and other animals; heavenly angels suspended from above; and a full-scale production of the first Christmas on a stage which by itself is bigger than some auditoriums. At Radio City Music Hall in New York City, following the high kicking of the renowned Rockettes, another Christmas pageant of breathtaking splendor unfolds daily for awestruck audiences. On TV the Grinch prepares to steal another Christmas, Charlie Brown to direct another

Christmas pageant, and Perry Como to croon his way through another family Christmas special.

These presentations add to the Christmas season an unmistakable element of showmanship, of drama, of light and color, but during the rest of the year they do not follow up by proclaiming what the first Christmas signaled, namely, the message of repentance and forgiveness of sins in Christ Crucified.

73

We may witness pageants right in our own churches at Christmas, pageants with various degrees of light and drama and feeling. Suzie as usual is as cute as a rosebud; Tony sings off-key; and little Maurice needs prompting with his part. We dim the lights for "Silent Night" and join in singing "Joy to the World" with an enthusiasm unequaled in our normal hymn singing. Some of us even choke back a sentimental tear or two as a warm glow settles over all, a feeling that belongs with children and giving and Christmas and the Christ Child.

Now I suppose you expect to hear, "Away with all the shiny lights, the scenery, the pageantry, the sentimentality!" No, that's not necessary. That is, unless you use those things as substitutes for the essential message of the birth of our Savior, unless you see only the lights that shine on the trees and ignore the light that must continue to shine for you daily, unless your pageantry means no more than a Radio City Music Hall seasonal revue.

God uses pageantry too. In the words leading up to our text Peter has just explained how he was privileged to see a real-life pageant on what he calls "the sacred mountain." The light of that pageant was the brilliant glory of heaven itself which enveloped and shone from the Lord Jesus. The participants were Moses and Elijah, making an earthly appearance to talk with Jesus. The narrator was God the Father, who identified Jesus as his own beloved Son in whom he was well pleased. The emotional impact was overwhelming.

So what does Peter make of it? He says it served to make "more certain" the "word of the prophets." Then he exhorts us to pay attention, not to the spectacular transfiguration, but to "the word of the prophets" "as to a light shining in a dark place." The Word that foretold the coming of the Christ Child sheds light in the darkness of this world. The Word that reveals Jesus as our Savior lights our way long after Christmas lights are packed away. In other words, let the pageantry enhance, rather than distract from, the Word.

Listen carefully as the Word tells you that Jesus born in Bethlehem is the promised ruler in Israel from everlasting. He is the Seed of the woman promised to Adam and Eve. Of him Isaiah had said, "The virgin will be with child and will give birth to a son" (7:14), and again, "He will be called Wonderful Counselor, Mighty God, Everlasting Father, Prince of Peace" (9:6). Of him Isaiah prophesied, "He was pierced for our transgressions, he was crushed for our iniquities" (53:5).

Faithfully follow the light of that Word, and look forward to yet another pageant when "the day dawns and the morning star rises in your hearts," when Jesus returns on the throne of glory and the angels sing and we are drawn to his eternal light.

Dear Jesus, shine in my heart and in my life by your Word, and let me each day rejoice to see the glory of your gospel. Amen.

27. I RELY ON THE BIBLE

Above all, you must understand that no prophecy of

Scripture came about by the prophet's own interpretation. For prophecy never had its origin in the will of man, but men spoke from God as they were carried along by the Holy Spirit. (2 Peter 1:20, 21)

75

We were sitting in a dormitory room at a public university — two freshmen matching wits. "It won't do you much good to study metaphysics," I challenged him. "God has to tell you how he made everything."

"I don't believe God has spoken directly to us," he shot back.

"I do — in the Bible."

"Nonsense! That's just some men's interpretation of what God is like."

"Not so! God inspired those men in order to show us the way to him. That's how he reveals himself to human beings."

"That's the way you see it. But others see it other ways. One person's opinion is as good as the other's. Everyone is trying to find the same God."

I don't know how long we argued, but you've just heard our unresolvable differences. To my friend the Bible was no more than the words of men interpreting the metaphysical forces at work in their lives. And my acceptance of their words was but one way among many of seeing the way to God.

My friend apparently hadn't ever read the words of our text. If he had, he had rejected them. Yet they stand to this day, clear and unchanged, and they will endure forever. They remind you and me, contrary to the opinion of the metaphysically minded college freshman and many like him, that we can rely on our Bibles. What's important is not how we see things, but how God shows them — not how we want things, but how God does them.

As far back as we can study the customs and mores of humankind, we see human beings trying to interpret the forces of divinity in their lives. Wherever life or force presented itself, there men were likely to see "god." No wonder, then, that we find gods and goddesses of war, of water, of love, of thunder and lightning in the traditions of most people. But was that the same sort of thing the prophets of Scripture were doing, except on a more sophisticated level — having somehow stumbled on the idea of one god behind all forces rather than many gods for many forces?

No, the evidence doesn't allow it. Those men received direct revelations from God in many instances. Paradoxically, those men often felt inadequate to "interpret" God and hesitated to speak for him. Moses tried to excuse himself as not being eloquent. Isaiah described himself as a man of unclean lips. Elijah thought he was the only believer left. Paul called himself the least of all the apostles. Whenever they went their own way, they found only trouble. So great a prophet as Moses didn't get to enter the Promised Land because he acted on what he saw instead of what God showed him. David didn't get to build the Temple. And in the New Testament era, who can forget the troubles Peter, who wrote our text, brought upon himself because he so often didn't see things the Lord's way?

What do you suppose the holy writers would have told us if they had reported things the way they themselves interpreted them, the way they wanted them to be? That's easy to guess. Actually we don't even have to guess. We know they would have directed us to look for an earthly kingdom of God, a true Camelot without any of the forces of evil to threaten it. And to find your place in the kingdom, you would have to earn it.

But these men did not tell us what *they* wanted; "they spoke from God as they were carried along by the Holy Spirit." We have their God-inspired words. Many pastors before me have tried to picture exactly how that worked —

always with some difficulty. We cannot adequately explain *how* the Holy Spirit "carried" the men along, but here we have God's assurance that his messengers expressed divine truths and did this with the very words God wanted them to use.

The Holy Spirit has shown us through Moses that the Seed of the woman would crush Satan's head, but be bruised himself in the process. The Holy Spirit has revealed through Micah that the expected King would be born in Bethlehem and through Isaiah that he would be born of a virgin. Through Isaiah he also revealed that men would reject and despise the King, through Zechariah that this King would enter Jerusalem riding a donkey, and through Isaiah that this holy King would die for us. Furthermore, the Holy Spirit has shown through David that the dead King would not rot in the grave.

A most unlikely Savior! Hardly the invention of men!

Finally, the Holy Spirit has shown you that you can trust your Bible because he has shown you the Christ of the prophets, Jesus Christ, your living Lord and King.

Father of mercies, in thy Word
What endless glory shines!
Forever be thy name adored
For these celestial lines.

Divine Instructor, gracious Lord,
Be thou forever near;
Teach me to love thy sacred Word
And view my Savior here.

Amen.

28. I STRIVE AGAINST FALSE TEACHERS

78

There were also false prophets among the people, just as there will be false teachers among you. They will secretly introduce destructive heresies, even denying the sovereign Lord who bought them — bringing swift destruction on themselves. Many will follow their shameful ways and will bring the way of truth into disrepute. (2 Peter 2:1,2)

Of all the warnings God issues in the Bible, which do you think he repeats most frequently? Is it the warning against drunkenness or the warning against sins of sex? Maybe you think it's the warning against the love of money or against the misuse of the tongue. In different ways, God warns many times against all of those things. I haven't made an actual count, but one warning, it seems, he repeats most often of all — the one that summarizes our text: "Beware of false teachers!" (cf. Matthew 7:15)

Why that one? And why is he so protective? Because this danger is ever present, so destructive and so contagious. That's a mouthful, so let's let Peter explain what it means.

The danger is ever present. Peter warns, "There were also false prophets among the people, just as there will be false teachers among you."

"There will be false teachers among you." Peter, remember, is writing to Christians, to you and me. Of course we can recognize false teachers out there somewhere, too far away to influence us directly — Moslems, Buddhists and hundreds of weird cults and sects. But we need to be looking also closer to home, where we can be touched and influenced, among our fellow Christians, indeed, even among the fellow Christians of our own beloved Lutheran Church.

Am I suggesting that we might actually have false

teachers in our own church body? It would be incredibly naive to suggest that it's impossible. But, no, I'm not thinking of anyone or accusing anyone in particular when I say this. In fact, with you, I'd like to believe that we, as a church, would immediately recognize any false teachers and dismiss them posthaste.

Ideally we would do just that, but in practice it's a tough job, for Peter says they bring in their heresies "secretly." The original language implies that false teachers bring in their false teachings "along side of" the true teachings so that we cannot always spot them easily. Consequently, while receiving the good, we may be receiving the bad right along with it, without knowing. It all looks good.

That begins to tell us why the danger is so destructive, too. It wears many disguises. It looks like the real pain killer, but it's laced with cyanide.

"Laced with cyanide?" Isn't that a bit extreme? Not if we believe Peter's inspired words. He calls the false teachings "heresies of destruction" and warns that the teachers are "even denying the Lord who bought them." They are attacking the very foundation on which our salvation rests.

Who does that? Who among Christians actually attacks Christ? For starters, those do who say, "Jesus saves," but deny that Jesus lives — I mean actually, bodily, in person, following his death. Those attack Christ who say, "Jesus saves," but add, so do Allah and Buddha and the gods of any other religions as long as their followers are sincere in their faith." Those oppose Christ who say, "Jesus saves," but mean only because of the perfect example he gave us for godly living. False teachings of that kind kill as surely as cyanide does, only with more lasting results — *everlasting*.

Texts like the one here scare me, because the danger they express is so contagious. "Many," Peter emphasizes, "will follow their shameful ways." And that makes me look around in my own church and ask, "Do we, too, sometimes fall in line?"

What, for example, is meant by the "shameful ways" of the false teachers? Surely it means following their false teachings. Yes, that and more, for the original expression here has unmistakable connotations of sensuality, of indecent conduct. It suggests that anytime we find it easy to act in a way that is a shame before God, we shame God and honor the ways of false teachers. We say by our actions that we don't have to listen that closely to all the teachings of God. We become like those who, say "Peace, peace, when there is no peace" (Jeremiah 6:14). That, I'm sure, raises a lot of questions for us and calls for much soul-searching.

So God warns and warns and warns. But for every warning against something God also offers an invitation to something better. Just as false teaching leads to destruction, so the true teaching leads to salvation in Jesus Christ who is the Way, the Truth and the Life. Turn, then, from all that is false; turn in faith to Jesus your Savior.

> Dear God of truth and mercy, turn us, we pray you, away from evil and always to the good, away from the false and always to the true, away from Satan and always to you, for Jesus' sake. Amen.

29. I NEED TO STAY ON THE WAY

If God did not spare angels when they sinned, but sent them to hell, putting them into gloomy dungeons to be held for judgment; if he did not spare the ancient world when he brought the flood on its ungodly people, but protected Noah, a preacher of righteousness, and seven others; if he condemned the cities of

Sodom and Gomorrah by burning them to ashes, and made them an example of what is going to happen to the ungodly; and if he rescued Lot, a righteous man, who was distressed by the filthy lives of lawless men (for that righteous man, living among them day after day, was tormented in his righteous soul by the lawless deeds he saw and heard) — if this is so, then the Lord knows how to rescue godly men from trials and to hold the unrighteous for the day of judgment, while continuing their punishment. This is exactly true of those who follow the corrupt desire of the sinful nature and despise authority. (2 Peter 2:4-10)

Can conservative Lutheran churches survive? Can we last into the 21st century with our spiritual moorings intact? Are we having an impact in the world even now?

"Strange questions," you say? Is it not true that conservative, Bible-believing churches are holding their own or even growing, while the more liberal denominations are generally declining in membership?

Yes, it's true. In my own ministry, I have seen two congregations in a geographic area multiply to twenty congregations in ten years, and that area has now been organized as a new synodical district. That typifies the way our work has been expanding in this country and abroad.

Why the foreboding questions, then? "Can we survive? Will we last? Are we having an impact?" Take another look. Many places where we ought to be sending new missionaries in our own country and in other lands, we hold back year after year because we don't get the money to finance the work. Meanwhile, it seems, fewer and fewer young people are interested in preparing for the ministry. As far as impact goes, do you realize that conservative Lutherans represent only a tiny minority of the population of our country?

Look again about you. Is the influence of the godly

prevailing? You know the answer as well as I. Today's prevailing attitudes are: Kill an unborn baby if it is an inconvenience. Pervert sexuality as long as you make your own choice. Use drugs and drink as you wish as long as it makes you feel good. Even praise God if you care to as long as you don't insist that he is real, personal and the only God.

More and more Christian churches are saying less and less about what is sinful. Our way is archaic, out of step with the times. We don't fit in today's way of life. We're still watching black and white TV and driving Model T Fords when compared to the pyrotechnical, rocket-propelled scene enveloping our society.

Can we survive?

Does it really matter? Is it worth the effort?

God, through Peter, is telling us today, "YES — we can, it does, it is." Just stay on the way; Christ's way, that is.

Sadly, the ungodly, as they sink even more deeply into the quagmire of immorality, become the archaic ones. The more blatantly people defy God, the more they become like the angels who sinned in the beginning, whom God confined to hell. The more they ignore the call of God, the more they resemble the ancient world which perished in the flood. The more they live for pleasure and sensuality, the more they look like Sodom and Gomorrah, which God burned to ashes.

We? We are Noah. We are Lot. God has reached us by his Spirit. He has shown us the way of Jesus Christ our Lord and Savior. He has rescued us from the world's corruption by directing his holy Son to the cross and the grave. He has declared us righteous with all men for Jesus' sake. And by grace through faith we walk in his way. Like Noah we have the message of salvation for the rest of the world, although many will not listen. Like Lot we are distressed and sometimes tormented by what we see and hear. But we stay on the way because God is with us.

Remember, God will punish the ungodly — in God's own way and in his own time. The judgment and hell await. God will rescue his people from the trials of this world. Heaven awaits.

Meanwhile, do we have an impact? For each new soul that repents and follows the way of Jesus in faith, the angels of heaven rejoice. Also, keep in mind, God would have spared Sodom and Gomorrah if only ten like righteous Lot had lived there. We can only wonder what he has done and will do for our country and this world for the sake of the righteous who live here.

May he always keep us in that number.

Dear heavenly Father, the ways of the ungodly seem to prevail and the ways of your people are threatened. Be with us, O God, so that we do not grow tired but rather work harder to spread the word of your way of salvation in Jesus Christ. Keep us on that way for Jesus' sake. Amen.

30. I NEED TO RESIST TEMPTATION

These men are springs without water and mists driven by a storm. Blackest darkness is reserved for them. For they mouth empty, boastful words and, by appealing to the lustful desires of sinful human nature, they entice people who are just escaping from those who live in error. They promise them freedom, while they themselves are slaves of depravity — for a man is a slave to whatever has mastered him. If they have escaped the corruption of the world by knowing our Lord and Savior Jesus Christ and are again entangled in it and overcome, they are worse off at the end than

they were at the beginning. It would have been better for them not to have known the way of righteousness, than to have know it and then to turn their backs on the sacred commandment that was passed on to them. Of them the proverbs are true: "A dog returns to its vomit," and, "A sow that is washed goes back to her wallowing in the mud." (2 Peter 2:17-22)

84

Them and us! In our two previous devotions, the inspired Peter directed us to take a look at them and us — at the false teachers opposed to us who follow the true ways of God, at the unrighteous opposed to us who find our righteousness in Christ, at the ungodly opposed to us in the family of God. Today he continues with the same kind of warning, denouncing the ungodly false teachers in no uncertain terms. But it isn't all "them and us," as if we are a breed apart and not susceptible to their ways. Instead Peter is warning against confusing them with us, warning that for us to become them is a tragedy of the worst order.

Never mind, for the moment, looking at those who threaten us with every perversion of God's Word and way. Look instead at yourself, for you are among those threatened. God has rescued you from the moral filth of this world. You "have escaped the corruption of the world," Peter says again here, "by knowing our Lord and Savior Jesus Christ." By faith in Jesus, you "have known the way of righteousness." You are a child of God.

But be careful! The gift of knowing Jesus as your Lord and Savior is not some toy to be trifled with. The "way of righteousness" is not some easy access highway to be exited and entered at will. You have a precious treasure in Jesus; guard it with your life.

It's not easy to resist temptations. Your own flesh likes what it hears from the panderers of pleasure and promiscuity. The world sells egomania and the religion of "me" with millions of dollars worth of commercials. The devil says he will set you free to fly like the birds, to float like the clouds. The false teacher offers you water to cool your fevered brow.

But then — the pleasure turns to pain. The more I love me, the less lovable I become. Freedom remains always beyond the next barrier. And the promised water turns to dust at the touch.

We walk a narrow path, a dangerous road.

By now, I wouldn't blame you if you were saying to yourself, "Ah, c'mon, now, loosen up a little. You know that everyone does some sinning. What's the big deal?"

Yes, I know that everyone sins. And like you, I cling to my crucified Savior for the forgiveness I require daily, but we also must guard against complacency.

God reminds us that every sin is an abomination that threatens to entangle us again in the slavery of depravity. He warns that when sin masters us we become the slaves of sin, caught and compelled to sin more and more, turning further from the Savior. The beginning of sinning is like beginning on a slippery slide that will deposit you on the garbage heap of worldliness. And when someone who has known the way of righteousness in Christ turns back to the way of corruption, it were better he had never known Jesus. He is like a dog returning to his vomit, a washed sow going back to wallow in the mud. He may never care to be clean again.

God has spoken. It's not just them against us. It's us determined in faith not to become them, not even to become a little bit like them, because that can be the first step to ruin. Resist the beginnings!

God, keep us steadfast in our faith.

Jesus, Savior, be with us as we walk on the way, longing for the day we reach our heavenly home with

85

you. Guide us by your Spirit that we may stay on the way of righteousness and never stray into the dark corruption of this world. Have mercy, O God. Help us now, even as you suffered and died to make your help available. Blessed be your name! Amen.

31. I LIVE IN THE AFTERGLOW OF EASTER

But do not forget this one thing, dear friends: With the Lord a day is like a thousand years, and a thousand years are like a day. The Lord is not slow in keeping his promise, as some understand slowness. He is patient with you, not wanting anyone to perish, but everyone to come to repentance. (2 Peter 3:8, 9)

Did you have a nice Easter? Never mind if you're reading this in the Trinity season or even in the Christmas season. Think back for the moment to your last Easter celebration. Did you on that day feel a sense of elation and of uncontained joy as you envisioned the exalted Savior bursting the chains of death and the grave? Do you remember also having a good feeling as you sat later in the afterglow of Easter? I know that's how it usually goes for me.

But now what if you are a long time removed from Easter, maybe weeks or months? Do you feel the same warmth and sense of Easter joy now? Or has the afterglow worn off and disappeared with time?

If the questions merely mean: "Will you be actively thinking much about Easter anymore in June?", I imagine it's safe to conclude that the afterglow will be gone. But if we take a more in-depth approach to the questions, we have reason to hope the good feeling will continue. For as Christians we live forever in the afterglow of Easter — not in the good feeling carrying over from last Easter Sunday's celebration, but in the certain hope of salvation made sure by the resurrection of Jesus Christ from the dead. He lives! Those two words undergird everything we hold dear as Christians.

Think about it. Have you received Holy Communion recently? What would the Supper mean if you couldn't say, "He lives"? Or what good would you get from praying in his name? What comfort when you are sick? What hope for a life better than this one? What relief from sin's guilt? What confidence that he is coming again on the Last Day —unless we know for sure that "He lives"?

We live in the afterglow of Easter. And the more you realize what that means, the better the feeling becomes.

Or does it? Whom are we kidding? Jesus reportedly rose from the dead how many hundreds of years ago? In the last thousand years or two — say since John the Apostle died — who has heard from Jesus? Meanwhile, just look at the shape the world is in. Never in all history has the future of mankind looked bleaker — with nation taking arms against nation and with the specter of a nuclear holocaust looming over the scene. Then, too, the only afterglow countless people care about is the good feeling they associate with self-indulgence and immoral living.

Still we insist, "Jesus lives." Why, then, does he allow things to go on as they are? What is he waiting for? Why is he delaying his reappearance? Where is he? After all these years, can we still believe he is alive and in control?

Those aren't my questions, you know. But the scoffers surely ask them — over and over again. And, left to our own human reason, we may not find it easy to answer. The Lord, therefore, through Peter gives us the only answers we need. They go something like this: In the first place, keep in mind, those who scoff are taking issue not with us, but with God, who created the heavens and the earth with his word and once already destroyed the earth in water. They argue with God, who has reserved the earth for a final destruction by fire. Then keep in mind that God is not bound by our concept of time. To the eternal Lord one day is like a thousand years and a thousand years are as a day. Furthermore, what we might consider needless delay is the patience of God, who holds back the Last Day in our interests. He does not want "anyone to perish, but everyone to come to repentance."

If you are at all close to the work of your church, you undoubtedly know that sinners are coming to repentance. Each time one does, you have reason to thank the Lord for not rushing the end. Right now, there is someone new in the bush of Africa learning of the Savior and someone else in Milwaukee, Wisconsin. God wants those people in his kingdom with you.

Meanwhile, the longer you live in faith and the more you live your life with Jesus at the center, the less sense the scoffers make. Maybe Jesus doesn't make a personal appearance to have you touch the wounds in his hands and side. But he stays close to you by the means of grace and makes his presence felt in your life. To be sure, the more you grow in your faith, the more you enjoy the afterglow of Easter. Jesus lives!

Dear Lord Jesus, our living Savior, thank you for keeping this world long enough so that we too may be counted among the penitent and can enjoy the afterglow of Easter. Keep us steadfast in our faith and lead those now living in unbelief to find their salvation with you while there is time. For your name's sake. Amen.

32. I LIVE FOR THE LIFE TO COME

The day of the Lord will come like a thief. The heavens will disappear with a roar; the elements will be destroyed by fire, and the earth and everything in it will be laid bare.

Since everything will be destroyed in this way, what kind of people ought you to be? You ought to live holy and godly lives as you look forward to the day of God and speed its coming. That day will bring about the destruction of the heavens by fire, and the elements will melt in the heat. But in keeping with his promise we are looking forward to a new heaven and a new earth, the home of righteousness.

So then, dear friends, since you are looking forward to this, make every effort to be found spotless, blameless and at peace with him. (2 Peter 3:10-14)

Are you tired of hearing from the pulpit all of the things you should or should not be doing day after day? Chances are that you can often guess what the preacher is going to say even before he says it. You know the list as well as I. He'll tell you to stop cheating; or avoid the temptation to cheat. Attend church regularly. Don't be a church skipper. Control your passions. "Flee the evil desires of youth" (2 Timothy 2:22). Watch out for booze. Control your tongue. Use God's name to bless and not to curse. Once in a while you'll hear a new angle, but as surely as you can recite the Ten Commandments, so surely you know what you should and should not be doing.

How then do you react to the exhortations? Do you pass them off as more of the same old thing and leave church untouched by any sense of urgency to do anything about them? Do you file them under things you ought to pay attention to someday? Do you think to yourself: "I wish my friend's roommate would listen to that," and fail to see how it fits into your own life? Do you feel there's plenty of time in the future to begin to clean up your act?

Clearly and sadly enough, knowing what is right and wrong does not assure that we will strive to do what's right and avoid what's wrong. In fact, what we know not to do we find ourselves doing; and what we know to do we find we don't do.

What does it all mean? It means — we surely do need our Savior. For every time and in every situation we come up short, he didn't. And his perfect life counts for us. For all the punishment we deserve from our faults, he suffered hell's fury on the cross for us. And we know it all counts because he rose from the dead.

It means also that without Jesus our living Savior, the coming destruction on the Last Day would seal our doom, and our insensitive carcasses would burn on that day and forever in hell.

Instead, because of Jesus we look forward to the Last Day and to "a new heaven and a new earth, the home of righteousness." And that tells us something again about how we ought to respond to the exhortations to godly living we outlined at the start. Peter by inspiration says, "You ought to live holy and godly lives as you look forward to the day of God." And he repeats, "So then, dear friends, since you are looking forward to this [namely, the new heaven and new earth with the Lord] make every effort to be found spotless, blameless and at peace with him."

Can you be indifferent to the call to godliness? I don't see how. Indifference is part of the process of hardening the heart. It wars against the very faith that connects you with Jesus. Your faith in Jesus, on the other hand, will prompt you to "make every effort to be found spotless, blameless." The question is no longer, "Can you achieve blameless-ness?" It's, "Will you strive in faith toward that goal?" Peter says, "Look ahead to what's waiting for you and do it."

Look at it his way: Jesus lives and walks with you in your life of faith. Act in a way that shows he is present. Jesus reigns in glory and will come to greet you bodily on the Last Day — when you least expect it. Live like someone expecting to greet the Lord in person in the next moment. Jesus offers you peace which the world cannot give. Walk always in peace. Jesus will restore a righteous world for you to enjoy in his presence. Strive for righteousness now. Jesus will help you.

Dear God, merciful Father, by the Spirit of your Son Jesus work in us the continuing desire to strive in faith to live a godly life here, even as we look forward to the life to come with you in heaven. We pray in Jesus' name. Amen.